# JOURNEYS IN
# THE KALI YUGA

"Often one has to travel far afield to the farthest edge to find out where one belongs. Aki Cederberg tells us the fascinating tale of his journey to the wild heart of mythical India, a journey that changed his life and led him back to his roots."

WOLF-DIETER STORL, PH.D., AUTHOR OF
*SHIVA: THE WILD GOD OF POWER AND ECSTASY*

"Cederberg has made the outer and inner journey from one end of the geography of tradition to the other, which is only an outer reflection of the inner journey many pilgrims make from the outer world to inner experience. What is remarkable about Cederberg's journey is that he, like Odysseus of old, found his way *home* again. The knowledge he gathered on his journeys gave him the tools he needed to discover the inner treasures of his own homeland. By reading this book you can gather some of this knowledge without ever going to India."

STEPHEN E. FLOWERS, AUTHOR OF *ORIGINAL MAGIC:*
*THE RITUALS AND INITIATIONS OF THE PERSIAN MAGI*

"From the erotic passion of Shiva to the surreal bliss of the Khumb Mela, Aki Cederberg chronicles his search for meaning in modern India. But, as he discovered, 'Pilgrimages have to come to an end. Ultimately, one *must* return home'—not just physically but spiritually as well. His story of how his own native European gods called to him is powerful, beautiful, irresistible. This book bears an important message for our times and delivers it in a way that captivates the reader. I recommend *Journeys in the Kali Yuga* without reservation."

STEPHEN MCNALLI
*ASATRU: A NATIVE EUROPEAN*

"Aki Cederberg is an outsider in the modern, spiritually barren \
for a sense of spiritual place takes him to the exotic East. There h
as well but is allowed something close to an insider's participat
pagan religious tradition. Instead of satisfaction, he finds only mc
for the largely forgotten traditions of his own people. Cederbei
which makes for a highly colorful, absorbing tale—functions
initiation into those traditions. It is a journey home."

COLLIN CLEARY, AUTHOR OF *WHAT IS A RUNE? AND OTHER ESSAYS*

# JOURNEYS IN THE KALI YUGA

## A Pilgrimage from Esoteric India to Pagan Europe

## AKI CEDERBERG

Destiny Books
Rochester, Vermont • Toronto, Canada

*369 5469*

Destiny Books
One Park Street
Rochester, Vermont 05767
www.DestinyBooks.com

Destiny Books is a division of Inner Traditions International

**Library of Congress Cataloging-in-Publication Data**
Names: Cederberg, Aki, 1978–
Title: Journeys in the Kali yuga : a pilgrimage from esoteric India to pagan
    Europe / Aki Cederberg.
Description: Rochester, Vermont : Destiny Books, 2017.
Identifiers: LCCN 2017019318 (print) | LCCN 2017040971 (e-book) |
    ISBN 9781620556795 (paperback) | ISBN 9781620556801 (e-book)
Subjects: LCSH: Cederberg, Aki, 1978- | Spiritual biography. | BISAC: BODY,
    MIND & SPIRIT / Mysticism. | BIOGRAPHY & AUTOBIOGRAPHY / Personal
    Memoirs. | TRAVEL / Asia / India.
Classification: LCC BL73.C373 (e-book) | LCC BL73.C373 A3 2017 (print) |
    DDC 204.092 [B]—dc23
LC record available at https://lccn.loc.gov/2017019318

Printed and bound in the United States by Berryville Graphics

10  9  8  7  6  5  4  3  2  1

Text design and layout by Virginia Scott Bowman
This book was typeset in Garamond Premier Pro with Titular and Avenir used as display typefaces

Photograph of Ganesh on page viii by A. Haapapuro

Figure 5.1, *Heathendom and Christendom* by Akseli Gallén-Kallela, reprinted by permission of the Finnish National Gallery/Ateneum Art Museum. Photo: Finnish National Gallery/ Hannu Aaltonen

To send correspondence to the author of this book, mail a first-class letter to the author c/o Inner Traditions • Bear & Company, One Park Street, Rochester, VT 05767, and we will forward the communication, or contact the author directly at **www.akicederberg.com**.

# CONTENTS

*Just as in the embrace of his beloved,*
*a man forgets the entire world,*
*all that exists within himself and without,*
*so in union with the Being of knowledge,*
*he no longer knows anything, either within or without.*

UPANISHADS

Om Shri Ganeshaya Namaha

# FOREWORD

## *For One Who Wanders Widely*

### By Michael Moynihan

IF THE HUMAN BEING is a *Homo religiosus* by nature, as so many signs suggest, then the impulse toward pilgrimage—a sacred journey or a journey in search of the sacred—must be nearly as old as the human sense of the higher powers themselves. The whole notion of pilgrimage assumes that divine forces are not restricted to a supernatural realm, solely accessible through worship or prayer, but instead may be found lingering in particular places here on Earth. These sites, marked by the gods and their most ardent devotees, may be numinous features in the natural landscape such as mountains, groves, trees, lakes, wells, and waterways, or man-made structures like temples, altars, and shrines. In many cases, natural and man-made elements are brought together to amplify and concentrate the spirit(s) of a place.

Sacred sites are remarkably resilient, thus demonstrating their innate power. They often maintain their special status despite the seismic shifts in external religious belief and custom that can occur with the passage of time. Even in the West—where the past few millennia saw earlier polytheistic worldviews replaced by monotheistic Christianity, which gave way to a muddleheaded modernism—sacred places can still be found dotted across the landscape. Some are as old as the Neolithic period.

Pilgrimage is an abiding feature of religions in the East and West. The Indian traditions of Hinduism and later Jainism recognize the action, *yatra* (pilgrimage), and the destination, *tirtha* (pilgrimage site or crossing-over place), terms that derive from ancient Sanskrit. Buddhists travel to the Mahabodhi Temple, the site of the bodhi tree under which Siddhartha Gautama attained enlightenment. For any able-bodied Muslim, a *hajj* (pilgrimage) to Mecca is a mandatory pillar of the faith. In pagan Scandinavia, the temple at Uppsala drew throngs of visitors who came from every part of Sweden to attend the great and bloody sacrificial feast that was held there every nine years. In late antiquity, Christians began making pilgrimages to the Holy Land. By the early Middle Ages, the city of Rome and its basilicas of the martyrs Peter and Paul had become a sacred destination for Christian pilgrims who traveled there from all parts of Europe and from as far away as Iceland. Common routes and roadmaps were developed for these pilgrimages, but the passages were beset with all manner of dangers. The journey itself would surely test a pilgrim's faith; successfully completed, the pilgrimage was a testament to the steadfastness of that same faith.

At the heart of pilgrimage, both the word and the concept, is the pilgrim, the one who boldly—and, in some cases, naively—undertakes such a venture. Etymologically, the word *pilgrim* derives from the Latin *peregrinus*, "foreigner," which in turn was probably formed from a combination of *per* ("through") and *ager* ("field," "land," or "terrain"). It thus signifies someone who travels, or has traveled, through a land.

In the case of Aki Cederberg's *Journeys in the Kali Yuga*, which recounts his ongoing quest for *darshan,* a "beholding" or direct view of the sacred, the destinations are literal and figurative, made of matter and spirit, and their pathways lead inward as well as farther afield. The pilgrimages that form the main backdrop of his account took place in

India, on far less beaten paths than those of the hajj or a journey to Jerusalem.

Navigating a terra incognita can be a disorienting experience on a metaphysical as well as a geographical level. This is certainly the case in a polytheistic land such as India, with its dense and deeply layered cultural and religious strata that have been accumulating and intermingling for millennia. Foreigners who travel there naively in search of some vague enlightenment and who lack a well-functioning internal compass may soon find themselves in an endless, hallucinatory labyrinth that confounds at every turn. As Cederberg observes, many return home "even more lost than they were when they first set out on their journey."

A large part of Cederberg's story tells of his initiation, and that of several other Europeans, into a lineage of Shaivite Naga Babas. His descriptions of these events and their surroundings are sincere, respectful, and colorful but devoid of romanticism. Despite his resonance with the ancient spiritual worldview of the Babas and his appreciation for the power of their rituals and customs, he eventually realizes he can never be truly at home in their world. No matter the length of the stay or the depth of the study, he is destined to remain a stranger in a strange land.

Cederberg's experiences in India serve as a hermetic and analogical catalyst on several levels. Along with a greater understanding of the sacred vertical correspondence "as above, so below" comes the recognition of a matching horizontal equation: "as within, so without." Just as the higher world of the gods has its parallel scenarios that play out perpetually here on Earth, an inner, mystical path has its equally valid outer, physical counterparts, such as the traditional martial arts. The analogy might be further extended to the world of the creative arts as a whole.

Most important of all, perhaps, Cederberg's encounter with the Shaivite Babas acts as a kind of magic mirror, the polished black surface of which forces the outsider, the viewer, to stare back into his own depths. The engagement with Hinduism leads not to an embrace of the exotic and a rejection of one's native roots—which in Cederberg's case have their mythic reference points in ancient Finnish and Germanic traditions—but to a renewed impulse to nourish those roots and, in turn, be nourished by them.

Western traditions do not provide the overwhelming plethora of gods and demigods that have coalesced in a culture such as India's, but this is not necessarily a bad thing. Our divinities and legendary heroes embody equally potent roles and functions—often in ways that are far more understandable to our psyches. And like an overgrown sacred site or a hidden holy well, they await an ongoing rediscovery. For most people in the modern world, making such rediscoveries—and really learning from them—demands a heroic effort. It is to this effort that Cederberg has dedicated a large part of his life.

In one of the aphoristic strophes from the Old Icelandic *Hávamál,* the god Odin warns that "wits are needed for one who wanders widely" (*Vits er þörf, þeim er víða ratar*). Cederberg has certainly wandered widely. He found entrancing and sometimes bewildering worlds to explore and crossed a few dark thresholds along the way. Thankfully, having kept his wits about him all the while, he has returned with a clearheaded field report from the spiritual front lines that is every bit as readable as it is relevant. *Journeys in the Kali Yuga* is much more than just a travelogue of intriguing tales. Taken together, the pilgrimages recounted in these pages tell a greater story.

Walpurgisnacht and May Day, 2017

Michael Moynihan is an author, translator, editor, and musician and holds a doctorate in Germanic philology. His nonfiction book *Lords of Chaos* (cowritten with Didrik Søderlind; revised edition, Feral House, 2003) has been translated into nine languages and is the basis for a feature film production. He has contributed to scholarly encyclopedias and topical anthologies, and coedits (with Joshua Buckley) the journal *TYR: Myth—Culture—Tradition*. Recent projects include the monograph *American Grotesque: The Life and Art of William Mortensen* (coedited with Larry Lytle) and a new edition of Mortensen's *The Command to Look* (both published by Feral House, 2014). As a translator, his work includes the annotated English edition of *Barbarian Rites: The Spiritual World of the Vikings and the Germanic Tribes* by Hans-Peter Hasenfratz, Ph.D. (Inner Traditions, 2011).

# WORDS OF POWER

## *A Translator's Foreword to an Untranslated Work*

### By Ike Vil

I AM A TRANSLATOR BY TRADE, or, perhaps more accurately, by accident. I dabble in other things, but one has to eat, too. I translate novels, biographies, articles, movies, and TV—everything except reality shows. That's where I draw the line, based on ethical grounds.

The first edition of this book was published in Finnish. It was, however, translated from English, as Mr. Cederberg wrote the original text, comprising chapters 1 through 4, for the excellent *Fenris Wolf* anthology. I translated it into Finnish and wrote the foreword. Now, rather than translate into English my Finnish foreword to a text that was translated from English—are you still with me?—it seemed to make more sense to start from scratch. Especially as the story continued beyond those initial chapters.

And that story is quite exceptional.

In the tradition of the best travelogues, it tells of strange, beautiful, and horrible things in distant lands where magic is not dead. For Westerners, it is a rare glimpse into an esoteric and often misunderstood tradition that challenges the way we see the world and ourselves. And it's not just about lurid anecdotes. The author actually brought back more than just a lousy T-shirt. For me, that is the greatest inspiration in this story.

They say that translating is something that should not be done, yet is still done. Despite some optimistic technocrats who think that machine translations will render humans redundant in a decade, most people understand that you can't really translate words—you can only translate ideas.

And that's where something is lost.

I first tried to make sense of the giddy world of magic in the mid-1980s, when, at the tender of age of fourteen, I got my hands on *The Book of Black Magic and of Pacts,* the classic late-nineteenth-century collection of Goetia by Arthur Edward Waite. Delving into the invocations, I started wondering about the wording of the litanies. Some words, like *Tetragrammaton,* which seemed to be Greek, were cool sounding, while others, like *Jehovah,* did not sound cool at all. And what about the English text accompanying those names in the invocations? Should I really chant the words in English for the rituals to work? This seemed a bit preposterous. Then I wondered if maybe I should use my native language, Finnish, instead, because I felt that, in any case, the magic should happen within myself.

Needless to say, the invocations didn't really work in any language—unless it was thanks to them that my life became this wonderful yet sometimes strenuous series of adventures.

I later found out about the words *gematria, notarikon, temurah, Qabbalah,* and *sephiroth*—there was a world of confusing analogy hidden in those Hebrew letters and numerals that I really didn't have a clue about. Still later, I started wondering if it's even my place to study the secrets of a hidden tradition of an alien culture that, as intriguing as it is, is not mine.

I could translate its ideas but not its words.

My heritage is that of the Elk-Folk, the Bear-Folk, the Tree-Folk, the mysteries of the woods and animals of the North.

Herman Melville wrote that "life's a voyage that's homeward bound." Like all meaningful truths, it probably sounds shallow at first. In our youth, we often go about parroting adages like that, things we profess to know about because we have read about them or seen them on TV. One of the few joys of getting old is that knowledge is tempered by our own experience and internalized. That's the alchemy that, at best, turns truisms to truths, or half-truths, at least. Ideally, we might learn to see where we used to only look; hear where we only listened; understand where we only read.

I am not an Indologist by any means, but even an ignorant, non-Vedic *mleccha* like me can appreciate how integral phonetics and syllables—the *words*—still are to the esotery in the world where Mr. Cederberg's story takes you. One colloquial Western definition of mantra is a "repetitive garble of meaningless words." How can the sacred syllable *Aum* then encompass the whole universe—its gods; birth, life, and death; plus fifty-one skulls in a garland that are actually letters?

It makes me sad to think that words, signs, and sounds probably used to have that kind of power in European cultures, too—literally, not figuratively. The letters in the Beith-Luis-Nin alphabet of ogham used to signify tree knowledge, too. And runes, oh man—I can't help thinking how the Finnish language is such a strange graveyard of words. The first known instance of the word *rune,* in the Einang stone, is *runo. Runo* still means "poem," but singing *runos* in *The Kalevala* actually means "casting spells." That is the kind of poetry that Robert Graves extols in *The White Goddess,* the only meaningful kind of poetry there is, one might argue. (I guess I should also mention that somebody has tried to remarry Finnish language with the matrikas he brought back from Goa: Ior Bock's [1942–2010] mythology is not for everyone, and I personally find it neither here or there, but there was a magnetism to his manner that only true poets and madmen possess.)

The unbroken oral tradition of the Elk-Folk and the Bear-Folk might be lost, the runos forgotten or mangled by later hands, but the *kantele* of Väinämöinen and the lyre of Orpheus are still there, waiting to be played. They're in nature, they're in our nature. We just have to find the words again. We have few holy men of our own to teach them anymore, to reveal to us the numinous in nature. We can't translate those words, only their meaning. We have to learn to read again. It can't be done by just thinking; it needs doing. Then maybe poets will once again become priests.

Unlike many others in search of the mythical East, I think Mr. Cederberg actually found what he was looking for. He went in search of magic mirrors and found them to be windows to a reality that is not outside but inside. That, too, sounds like a truism. But maybe all pilgrimages really are voyages that lead us home.

I'm looking forward to the continuation of Mr. Cederberg's story, the story he wanted to find, the story he wanted to become.

It is a story in all of us, and of all of us, but it is written with a magical alphabet.

PORVOO, FINLAND
SEPTEMBER 2016

IKE VIL, M.A., is a Finnish musician, writer, and translator. His current band Sleep of Monsters recently released an album called *Poison Garden* (Svart Records, 2016). He's currently writing a historical novel.

# ACKNOWLEDGMENTS

Thank you:

Shri Mahant Rampuri, Shri Mahant Mangalanand Puri and Surendra Puri, and all the Babas and sadhus, named and unnamed, of the Juna Akhara and beyond.

Ike Vil, Michael Moynihan, Carl Abrahamsson, Savitri Puri, Yogananda Puri, Vijaya and Lars, Christian Möllenhoff, Antti Haapapuro, Matti Rautaniemi, Justine Cederberg.

Jon Graham, my editor Laura Schlivek, Jeanie Levitan, Manzanita Carpenter Sanz, Erica B. Robinson, Patricia Rydle, Jill Rogers, and everyone else at Inner Traditions who has worked on the present book.

My mother, Anneli Kangas-Cederberg.

All fellow travelers and seekers, present and far away, with whom the journey has been shared.

*A Decade*

# INTRODUCTION

AS FAR BACK AS I CAN REMEMBER, I have been drawn to and felt a strong resonance with certain sights, symbols, and signs, not exactly knowing why and perhaps more intensely than many of those around me. Some of these have been found in the waking world, while others have revealed themselves in visions and dreams. Many are far enough in the distant past to be in the realm where memory, dream, and waking reality all meld together in one amorphous mass of consciousness. As a result, through the whole of my life, I have been guided by some indefinable force that has propelled me toward these things and their revealing and realization.

Some of these dreams have been of such majesty that they have never left me, becoming mental talismans or maps of inner landscapes I have sought to find, even if I cannot remember exactly where I have seen them. In one such childhood dream, I wake up in a bed in the middle of a strange temple, the pillars of which rise up monolithically against the roof somewhere beyond sight. There is primal music echoing in the large circular hall, perhaps played by some kind of organ, that creates a surreal sonic harmony. As I scale its walls I discover it has neither doors nor windows, and one cannot exit or enter—one simply is there. Nevertheless, I feel as if I have arrived at the source of all and feel at home in this strange place.

In another later dream, I descend through the sea in a spherical vessel, arriving at a cave-like underworld shrine to primal, undivided truth and knowledge. There is an altar on the main wall on which shines a rune that I understand to be a synthesis of a mark for fire and a mark for ice. Surrounding the rune are innumerable small black-and-white framed pictures of people who have grasped and expressed this knowledge in their life and work.

Ever since realizing these and other dreams and visions, I have sought their equivalent in the waking world. It's as if my soul or spirit had been imprinted with images, and consequently my life has been a search for these images in the outside world, applying the hermetic axiom "as above, so below" to "as within, so without." Rather than looking for truths or meanings stemming from outside of myself, it has been an inward quest to find and to make manifest deep inner truths—truths perhaps not found in books, ideas, theories, ideologies, religions or "isms," but in living reality. In essence, I have been in search of magic mirrors.

I have also always had a strong wanderlust, a great thirst for journey, for travel, for quest and adventure. I have sat on the shores of the great, vast ocean and felt the waves bring with them a sense of restlessness, of faraway places, of grand discoveries—a calling and a longing for some distant land beyond the horizon. Perhaps it is in my blood, my ancestral seafarers and sea gods beckoning me, calling me out into their realms.

All of this in turn has taken me on journeys across the Earth, on pilgrimages to worlds above and below, and needless to say, to some very strange alleyways. The story that follows is of one such pilgrimage, consisting of a series of journeys to an extraordinary world where—in the face of our evermore secular and modern world in which ancient living lines of knowledge and magic are broken and severed forever—an ancient line of knowledge and magic is still alive.

# 1
# PILGRIMAGE

MANY YEARS AGO, I traveled across India and Nepal for several months. I was on a magical mystery tour, ranging from north India to the south and back again, all the way to Nepal, crossing the lands from one sacred site to another. In retrospect I can see how little books had portrayed the reality of things, and as a consequence, how lost I was momentarily. However, there are few things as edifying as direct experience, and the journey in all its uneasy glory and magical momentum certainly was that for me. As I look into that time and place in the past, it all comes back to me in a whirlwind of moments, as a surreal mixture of deep depths and great heights.

Travel in India can sometimes be an overwhelming, even psychedelic experience. Everything in that ancient land, where modernity is still at pains in the shadows of old gods, is multiplied and manifold—people and things, sights and sounds, joy and suffering. To be confronted directly with the wide spectrum and reality of life and death, of sublime, majestic beauty and power, as well as horrific suffering and ugliness (sometimes hand in hand), is not something we Westerners are necessarily used to. We quickly become aware of our cultural biases and how much they shape, limit, and inform our view of the world, whether we like it or not. Yet over time, things start to unfold in a different manner. Beyond the apparent confusion and chaos, a strange, subtle, and almost comical order begins to reveal itself, where things, despite contrary appearances, somehow happen.

And so there were strange, turbulent times. Life out of balance in hellish, overcrowded, methane-smelling metropolises, and in shitty, surreally poor villages. The never-ending slums, the shacks and huts in the dirt, the bolted doors of temples. People literally living in public toilets. The constant screams, screeches, and car horns. The everyday explosions of bombs made to either destroy or delight. Terrorist attacks in crowded markets and busses. In the evening news, angry, despairing faces and blood on the streets. The endless barking dogs under gray, polluted skies where no stars are visible. The hecklers, beggars, thieves, amputees, the bereaved children with deeply set, dark eyes. The legless, leprosy-ridden human creatures shuffling around in carts made out of cardboard boxes. I remember one of them in particular, who some American travelers called the "sucking ass-wound boy."

In Delhi, deranged with dengue, I had fever dreams imbued with images of Kali. Later, as I sat in a hospital, I watched actual birds fly inside the main hall. The doctor told me that my blood values were all over the place but finished with an overly happy smile and the mandatory Indian mantra, "Don't worry sir, everything is all right"—even when it clearly was not all right.

During the festival of Navratri (Nine Nights), celebrating the Goddess in her various forms, the streets were lined with statues of the fierce goddess Durga. Concluding the festival was Dussehra, which celebrated the victory of the god Rama over the demon Ravana. In a field in Faridabad, a slum of Delhi, three gigantic statues of demons filled with explosives were shot at with burning arrows by guys dressed as gods. The statues exploded and crashed to the ground with a force suitable to that of demons. The air filled with smoke and screams; the sky rained burning bits and ash. The gathered masses ran madly around the blazing, crumbling fire statues, the scene reminiscent of some dreamlike drunken war. Pushing through the multitudes, I felt the stare of thousands of eyes, while the police were exercising crowd control with unmerciful blows of their canes.

At the insistence of an Indian friend, and out of morbid curiosity, I visited the local center of the International Society for Krishna Consciousness (ISKCON), commonly referred to as the Hare Krishna movement. This movement, so popular in the West, is a watered-down, Christianized, modern Hindu sect that has made Krishna into its Jesus. Consequently, it has very little to do with ancient lines of knowledge. At the center, the statues of the mighty Indian gods were made out of cheap-looking plastic. My ears hurt as the loudspeakers were turned up way beyond their capacity and blared out the distorted mantra central to the Hare Krishna followers. Despite their claims, the repetition of this mantra was not the answer to everything.

Later on, traveling in Nepal with a friend, somewhere between Kathmandu and Pokhara, there was the young girl who had a seriously scarred-up face and one blind eye but was clearly and eerily beautiful beneath all the scars. She was collecting signatures and donations for who knows what in the bus we were on. We did not sign or give her anything, being weary from all the traveling and the never-ending line of people asking, begging, and hustling for money. Suddenly there was a commotion between the young girl and the driver of the bus. The girl struggled but got violently thrown out of the bus, hit in the head, and kicked in the chest. She was left crying at the stop as the bus drove off. We later learned from the only other Westerners on board that the commotion was apparently because she had dropped something on the floor of the bus and was trying to retrieve it. That treasured something turned out to be a ballpoint pen.

To counter the sometimes heavy experiences one inevitably had, it seemed reasonable to counteract those with *other kinds* of heavy experiences. The nightlife in Kathmandu was nonexistent because of the frequent curfews and shut-downs, and so it happened one night that we were strolling down an empty street, looking for a place to have a drink, when we encountered an underground place that seemed to be open. There was a doorman of some kind who smiled and waved us in. As we descended to the floor beneath the ground below, we quickly realized what the place was: a Nepalese strip joint, or at least it resembled one, except that the girls on stage did not actually strip but simply danced around to weird Nepalese disco music. Never having been ones to shy away from the seamier side of life, we sat down and ordered a full bottle of whiskey. We were immediately joined by three or four prostitutes, smelling the money, and the whiskey bottle was finished in about five minutes. One of the older and less-good-looking girls was trying to grab my crotch under the table, her lipstick-smeared mouth slobbering in my ear, "I want you, English dick." As I talked to a young, beautiful Indian-looking girl, I thought of the high prevalence of HIV among female sex workers in Nepal. Having had enough of the whiskey, the pushy prostitutes, and the somewhat sinister and sordid air of the place, I gave some money to the young girl, and we left for the night and the deserted streets.

A few days later we were supposed to visit the studio of the Thangka* painter Surendra Bahadur Shahi, a contributor to the book *Shamanism and Tantra in the Himalayas*,[†] but a soldier had shot several civilians, which resulted in a general strike. The guesthouse proprietor warned us against going out into the streets, but we went anyway. The mood was tense, fearful, and filled with soon-to-erupt violence. Everything was closed. All public transportation had been stopped. People marched and screamed down the streets, and in places menacing soldiers and army vehicles gathered. Outbursts of violence against the army by civilians and students had already erupted in other parts in Nepal, so the situ-

---

*Thangka is a Tibetan and Nepalese tradition of elaborate painting on cotton or silk appliqué, depicting Hindu or Tibetan Buddhist deities or mandalas. More than mere decorative art, Thangkas have a function in ritual, meditation, and monastic life.
†Claudia Müller-Ebeling, Christian Rätsch, and Surendra Bahadur Shahi, *Shamanism and Tantra in the Himalayas* (Rochester, Vt.: Inner Traditions, 2002).

ation looked grim. When we returned to the guesthouse rooftop, we bumped into a familiar American traveler sitting by a plastic garden table that held books, incense, and a small glass pipe for his dope. He was on his way, via Varanasi, to someplace to participate in a course in yoga, meditation, or something along those lines. Soon we were joined by another somewhat weary traveler from Australia. He had been traveling for three years straight and was a little paranoid, and later went into a long monologue about ley lines. Indeed it seemed most young Western people in Nepal were into strange theories and esoteric practices in one way or another—the Californian hippy influence was undeniable.

We decided to drink the day away on the rooftop and called out for beer and Royal Stag whiskey. Down below, angry mobs were pacing up and down the streets. As the day slowly melted into night, our little bacchanalia escalated to involve sudden vomiting; lapsing into trance; actions involving cigarette burns, mantras, and gongs; and more whiskey, much to the bewilderment of nearby neighbors. At one point the American was dangling on the edge of the rooftop, and I pulled him violently back to safety, which resulted in yet more broken pottery and legless plastic garden furniture. As night arrived and the restlessness of the streets finally died down, we managed to create a chaos of our own on the rooftop, and there was something truly reckless and apocalyptic in the air.

Seeking the sacred, one often found death instead. Death, which is so omnipresent and out in the open in much of India and Nepal, is treated in a fashion diametrically opposed to that of the West. There is much less of the sentimentality and taboo associated with death that characterizes the Western relationship with it. As a young man said to me in Nepal: "Family don't pay so much emotion here because we believe destruction means creation. So we are not scared of dying, more scared of karma."

There was a constant smell of shit and incense in the air in Varanasi, the city of Lord Shiva, the city of death and the eternal city of light, and a city of thieves and holy men, with labyrinthine alleys and ancient temples, where people came to die—a restless city that never slept. At night colorful, psychedelically lit parades meandered through the streets as the *aarti puja,* the ancient fire ritual,* was performed by the holy river Ganga (Ganges). And the Ganga, the central vein and holy mother of India, was itself the source of all this life and death, being perfectly pure and simultaneously utterly contaminated, reflecting the ever-present paradoxes in India.

We were sitting at the Manikarnika Ghat† by the Ganga, watching the bodies being cremated as the sun rose. As I raised my gaze skyward, the air filled with drifting, floating pieces of ash, while flocks of birds flew overhead. This was one of Lord Shiva's favorite dancing grounds, where they say the fire of the *dhuni,* the sacred ritual fire, has not died out in thousands of years. At dawn and dusk a serenity, a strange calmness, seemed to overtake the ghat as the air was warmed with the smell of endless human barbeques. Trampling on a piece of charred human bone amid the golden rays of the dawn, a dark casteless man said, "Burning is learning—all is ash" (see color plate 1).

In Nepal by the holy Bagmati River, at the cremation ghats of Pashupatinath, one of the largest temples to Shiva in the world—in his form as Pashupati, "lord of animals"—we again watched bodies, wrapped in golden shrouds, burn, as the *pandits* (Brahmin priests) performed the last rites. As in Varanasi, they used a special kind of rosewood for the funeral pyres so the bodies did not to give off a foul smell when burning.

Nearby was the tantric Bachhareshwari Temple, dedicated to Shiva's consort Parvati, with paintings and carvings of dancing skeletons and erotic, copulating figures. In ancient times during the Shivaratri festival, human sacrifices were performed here, at least according to our

---

*Puja* means "ritualistic reverence or worship."
†A *ghat* is a flight of steps leading to a body of water.

young guide. We visited the burial ground of the *sadhus* in the nearby forest and saw some of their dwelling places—caves and huts in the wall of a cliff.*

Later we wandered down to Ram Ghat, again by a river, where the poorer classes are burned. Here, however, there were no temples, no ghats, and no pandits, and it looked more like a construction site than anything else. A family had gathered to perform their last rites. Somewhat unceremoniously, the body was laid out and burned, but instead of fine, pleasant-smelling rosewood, they used car tires, creating a thick, black, acrid smoke.

I woke up before dawn in the only guesthouse of the tiny village of Pharping, Nepal. Here life was quiet, except for each Tuesday and Saturday when the local Dakshinkali Temple attracted pilgrims from all over the Kathmandu Valley, and a spiritual and sacrificial frenzy took over. I curled up in my sleeping bag and had some whiskey and a cigarette while watching the sunrise over the Himalayas. A young woman walked up a path carrying a heavy load on her back. Slowly the sounds of the arriving buses of pilgrims became more and more prevalent in the distance.

Dakshinkali Temple itself is situated in a cleft between two hills at the confluence of two rivers. The temple is dedicated to the great mother goddess Kali, the Shakti of Lord Shiva, in her ferocious, wrathful form (see color plate 2). The main deity in the temple is the black, six-armed, stone figure of Kali, standing on a prostrate figure (Shiva). Twice a week, a steady parade of animal sacrifices—chickens, ducks, sheep, and goats—are offered to her.

As we wandered down to the temple, the air echoed with hymns to Kali being played from the loudspeakers. Entire families lined up to have a chance to make a sacrificial offering in the main temple enclosure,

---

*Sadhus are mystic holy men who have renounced worldly life.

which we as Westerners, and hence non-Hindus, had no access to. But as it was an open temple with neither walls nor roofs, we could stand and witness the sacrificial procession in silence. The animals were quickly and unceremoniously slaughtered by professional butchers, after which the carcasses were taken to be cleaned, cooked, and prepared for dinner right beside the temple. After the sacrifices, families gathered in the woods and hills nearby for picnics.

Journeying across India and Nepal, visiting more shrines and holy places than I could recollect here, I began to notice that nature is "marked." The holy places were not random or arbitrary but situated in conjunction with some natural landmark: a river, lake, mountain, or tree. All of nature is considered holy, being the manifestation and dwelling place of gods and spirits. Mountains are gods, the rivers goddesses. Lakes, trees, caves, and indeed all forms of life and creation are likewise thought of as being embodied with spirits, the personalities of nature, whether benign or malevolent. And all of these elements seem to be connected by the three ever-present holy rivers of India—the Ganga, the Yamuna, and the invisible, mythic Saraswati.

Beyond the landmarks was something perhaps even more visceral: the real living human beings, far removed from the norms and conventions of modern life and society, still carrying along an ancient esoteric tradition and way of knowledge. I wanted to meet these crazy magicians, these sadhus, yogis, and shamans—*Babas* as they are affectionately called—who still inhabit this ancient land, be they hucksters or miracle men. Emulating their patron gods Shiva or Vishnu, they took on the appearance and attributes of those gods, thereby becoming living idols. In the case of Shiva, the appearance and attributes were wild. With their long *jata* (matted locks of hair) reaching to the ground, wearing *malas* (rosaries) made out of the seeds of the Rudraksha tree, adorned with flower garlands, sometimes skyclad and smeared in ashes, and carrying *trishuls* (tridents of Shiva), the sadhus were an awe-inspiring sight. They were spiritual outsiders, both respected and

Fig. 1.1. Animal sacrifice at Dakshinkali
(Photograph by A. Haapapuro)

feared, givers of blessings and throwers of curses. Looking at pictures of them, and later meeting them in person, I noticed something feral in their eyes, a look of power, fearlessness, and pride. They seemed to possess something that could not be taken away, but then what can be taken away from someone who has given up everything? Or perhaps something possessed *them*.

And yet, although the sacred was everywhere, approaching it as a foreigner was never quite as easy as it might seem in theory. One rarely found what one expected. The sadhus one saw in cities and famous temples were often clearly fakes: thieves, hucksters, and criminals on the run, whose ochre robes were just a little bit too brightly orange, having donned the sadhu look in order to evade prosecution or con gullible people out of their money. Sometimes, one would see them walking along roadsides or loitering at tourist destinations. One mark of a real sadhu was that they, having renounced the ordinary world, had very little reason to come to you for anything; you had to go to them. In Varanasi, colorful, questionably social sadhus were often wandering around or sitting by the river, sheltered from the sun.

Also in Varanasi, I visited the Baba Keenaram Sthal, the central ashram of the dreaded and infamous Aghori sadhus, known for their taboo-breaking, nefarious spiritual practices. The ashram was decked out in large skulls, but the sadhus themselves were nowhere to be seen. Apparently, they were fond of dwelling at cremation grounds and shouting swear words at everyday folks.

The first time I met what may have been a genuine sadhu was at Pashupatinath, Nepal, attending a small aarti puja at the hut of a local Naga Baba, "naked one" (a sadhu belonging to a specific order), which was situated right behind the platforms on which bodies were burning. The Naga Baba, ash clad and naked save for a loincloth and mala beads, was shouting at the top of his lungs with an authoritative and somewhat mad voice, constantly taking deep tokes from a *chillum* (a pipe for smoking cannabis and sometimes other plant substances), only pausing occasionally to vomit into a bowl. The air in the low-roofed room was thick with smoke from the dhuni, the incense, and the *charas* (cannabis) (see color plate 3). A young priest wearing a Britney Spears T-shirt conducted the puja, and the incessant loud beating of the *ghantas* (bells), the blowing of the conch-shell trumpet, and the rhythm of double-headed *damaru* drum in tandem with the intoxicated chants to Shiva provided a trance-inducing experience . . . at least until Baba's cell phone rang—with the famous Nokia ringtone, of all things.

Having traveled halfway around the planet from the "land of Nokia" to find connections beyond cell phones and hearing that ringtone at the feet of this divine madman, I need not tell you of the surreal irony of the situation.

In the end, we put some money under the Baba's feet, and he blessed us with smatterings of *vibhuti* (sacred ash) on our foreheads. As we left for the night, we were told by our young guide that the Naga Baba in question performs *tapasya,* austerities to get the attention of god, by lifting weights of up to 220 pounds with his penis. "But only in graveyards," our guide continued with a smile. "You need to have a very strong cock."

I took in these experiences, all the life and death, all the heights and depths—perhaps more than could be digested into knowledge in such a short time. But I began to wonder about the significance of all these things—the strange rituals on rooftops of empty monasteries, the reveries at shrines to unknown gods, the revelations of the extraordinary in unexpected moments and places. Beyond the exotic, what did I really think I was going to find as a foreigner in these strange lands?

I was seeking *darshan,* the "beholding," a vision and a direct revealing of the sacred. Rather than information gained from books or secondhand sources, darshan implies being personally touched by this revealing. But sadly, I often felt far removed from such an experience by the harsh realities of life in India. Even at holy places, at natural enclaves, in temples, at spiritual festivals, and when meeting supposedly holy men and receiving their blessings, I often felt detached. I heard there were supposed to be 300 million gods in India—and yet I could not find a single one.

Then in another moment, through the dirty window of a bus, I would see a giant statue of the god Shiva standing above all the urban rubble, the smog, shit, and suffering, in blissful serenity against an orange sunset. In those moments, something would be stirred within me, and I would remember.

And so there were times when this great *something* would reveal itself in small but profound glimpses. It was as if I had suddenly and almost accidentally pierced the veil of some grand illusion and arrived stumblingly at the source of it all. These were unexpected moments of revelation, of ecstasy and joyful wisdom, moments of a god drunkenness. In these moments I sometimes thought of the mantra *Om Shivoham* ("I am Shiva!") and envisioned myself *as* Shiva, and I could sense all around me as manifest divinity, as Shakti.

In the Himalayas of northern India, I made a pilgrimage to a *mandir* (temple) at the top of a mountain. The temple had no walls or roof, only pillars and altars supporting hundreds of bells that echoed across the ranges—hence its name, *Ghoda Khal,* which I understood to mean simply "bell temple." Beyond the pillars were the majestic mountains stretching into all directions. I thought of the line from some gnostic text—maybe the Gospel of Thomas—"God does not live in a building," and never was this more evident than here. The friendly pandit wanted to do a personal blessing puja for me and so we sat at the shrine of a local god, while the drummer banged away on his drum and the pandit conducted the puja, blowing the conch-shell trumpet and reciting mantras. As I began my slow descent down the mountain I soon sat down to marvel at the breathtaking vistas surrounding me, realizing why these mountains are thought to be the home of Shiva and indeed how mountains are the celestial home of the gods in virtually all cultures.

Fig. 1.2. A statue of goddess Kali Ma on top of a mountain temple,
at the feet of which regular animal sacrifices are performed
(Photograph by the author)

Beyond the polluted harbor of Mumbai lies the ancient island of Elephanta. On the island are several caves dedicated to various gods, cut into solid rock some 1,300 years ago. Unfortunately but not surprisingly, many of these ancient and impressive sculptures are in terrible shape not because of their age but because of the sabotage and plunder of man: after being ruled by several Hindu dynasties, the island eventually fell to the sultans of Gujarat and passed from them to the Portuguese soldiers, and the rest, as they say, is history.

The main cave on the island is dedicated to Lord Shiva, and despite being a major tourist attraction it still echoes with timeless and awe-inspiring beauty and power. It is a complex structure featuring Shiva in his many varied forms, as well as his consort, Shakti, and his family and entourage, including his elephant-headed son, Ganesh. There is the main shrine guarded on all sides by the protective *dwarapalas,* wherein one finds a Shiva *lingam* (a phallus-shaped rock) and *yoni* (a vulva-shaped rock at the base of the lingam)—the self-evident symbols of creation and unity.

Despite the thousands of ancient statues and monuments in celebration of sacred sex, where people are copulating in every possible manner, despite the central religious symbols of the phallus and vulva, modern India is very prudish and moralistic in its approach to sex, and many of its esoteric traditions are still strongly linked with abstinence and renunciation. For a country whose ancient history is so steeped in an appreciation of divine Eros, it seems as if something has been forgotten. Standing in the shadows of these ancient structures and laying hands on the lingam, I was reminded of something I read in a book by French historian, philosopher, musicologist, and Western convert to Shaivite Hinduism, Alain Daniélou:

> Shiva is the principle of erotic pleasure, not of fecundity. Wandering
> in the forest, he spreads his sperm by masturbatory practices and
> inspires desire and erotic madness.... All the beauty and all the joy

Fig. 1.3. Shiva lingam shrine, guarded in all directions by
the dwarapalas, Elephanta Island, Mumbai
(Photograph by the author)

in the world is manifested by means of an erotic explosion. Flowers cast their pollen to the wind. . . . The creation of the world is an erotic act, an act of love, and everything which exists bears this sign and this message. In living beings, everything is organized in accordance with this expression of pleasure, joy, beauty and happiness, which is the nature of the divine and the secret of all that exists. Eroticism is the bond of attraction uniting two opposite and complimentary poles.*

In Goa, intoxicated by the full moon and Royal Stag whiskey, I danced under a massive, psychedelically lit Shiva Nataraja statue as the waves of the Arabian Sea crashed ashore. A *bindu* (point) of blood on my third eye, I was clothed all in white and glowed in the darkness, as did Shiva Nataraja, dancing his eternal dance of creation and destruction. There in the darkness I felt something primordial slumbering and divine madness, drunkenness, desire. Perhaps it was the serpentine goddess Kundalini, and I was worshipping her golden skin and flowing like silver on her surface.

Shiva is the god of criminals and cops, artists and outsiders, rather than of householders, businessmen, and the status quo. He attracts marginal elements and creatures that live beyond the ordinary, at the edges, beyond the normative rules of reality and society. In this sense I was no exception: not a cop or criminal, but an artist of some kind, and an outsider most certainly. Shiva was the ultimate outsider, and he lived here in these strange lands that I found myself in. Is it any wonder that he spoke to me?

The sign of Shiva—the trishul—was very reminiscent of the trident-like Algiz rune (ᛉ) that I have as a talismanic tattoo on my arm, made when I was very young. Indeed it seemed to mark and point to similar areas and was one example of how things resemble each other in

---

*Alain Daniélou, *Gods of Love and Ecstasy: The Traditions of Shiva and Dionysus* (Rochester, Vt.: Inner Traditions, 1992), 157.

a deeper way. And what had brought me here was exactly that: resemblances and similarities. There were things in the world that approximated each other, that seemed to be similar or related in mystical ways, that seemed to mirror each other beyond even the cultural differences and forms. For me there seemed to be a common thread running through it all, a current running invisibly through separated streams, connecting them. It was these things that attracted me: the things that instinctively spoke to me, primal images that had always resonated with me and that alluded to an underlying unity.

There was also a living context and tradition, a way of upholding and obtaining esoteric knowledge, rooted in primeval sources that stretched back to some of the oldest surviving civilizations of mankind. I saw it as a pagan tradition reflecting an ancient line of knowledge, not yet broken and springing from the dawn of consciousness to the present age. It was something that had withstood, at least partially, the ultimate test: the test of time. And at the center of all of this seemed to hover perhaps one of the oldest continually revered gods in the world: the mystical figure of Shiva.

Shiva is pure consciousness. He is Adi Nath, "First Lord," the pure consciousness and ultimate reality at the core of all beings and things. The seemingly endless litany of his different names give form to his infinite qualities and supreme, all-pervasive nature. In his being, Shiva transcends all dualities; in his contrasting qualities he points to the principle of unification.

Shiva is Ardhanarishvara, the hermaphrodite deity, both male and female, signifying that god is a unity of the masculine and the feminine elements of the universe, as Shiva unites with Shakti. Shiva is Shankara, the primordial yogi, the great ascetic of the highest mountains, where he resides in inward-turned isolation and silence, as motionless, nonexpansive, still consciousness. Shiva is Nataraja, "king of the art of dancing," the moving, ever-expansive consciousness, engaged in an endless dance of creation and destruction. Shiva is Rudra, the terrible, the howler, the

Fig. 1.4. Shiva Nataraja in the eternal dance of creation
and destruction, surrounded by his divine
entourage, Elephanta, Mumbai
(Photograph by the author)

lord of tears. Shiva is Nandikeshwara, lord of joy, and Pashupati, the wild god of the animals and wild beasts.

To redeem the world, Shiva drank the poison of the world, which turned his throat blue, and thus he is Nilakantha, "the blue-throated one." To cool the burning sensation of the poison, he was given the moon, which he still wears in his hair. Indeed, he is purported to have said that there is still much poison in this world, which only heroes can drink, wherefore Shiva is the god of all intoxicating substances. Nothing is foreign to Shiva; he is boundlessly merciful and accepts all, and so he is Bholenath, the kindhearted lord, "protector of gawks and geezers."

Shiva is rich beyond rich, yet clothed in tiger skins, ashes, garlands of skulls and serpents, holding horns and trishuls, accompanied by his entourage of heavenly hooligans and rowdy spirits, the *ganas*. He is the lover of lovers, who copulated with his lady of the mountains, Parvati, for thousands of years. He is the lord of sensual delights and an ascetic, and he is simultaneously the lord of life and death, creation and destruction.

His third eye, once open, both destroys and creates the world. Shiva is Lord of the Three Worlds and of past, present, and future, as his forehead is marked by three horizontal lines of ash. And yet he is without beginning or end; he is a pillar of fire that penetrates all worlds.

His sign is the lingam, the cosmic principle of creation in the form of the phallus, standing erect in the yoni, the female receptacle, marking the divine interplay of Shiva (consciousness) and Shakti (energy, matter, and all manifestation), as well as the synthesis of the male and the female, and indeed of all polarities.

Shiva is a god wholly different in nature from those of the other major world religions, or even from those of most modern recreations of some ancient sects. Shiva is a totality, incorporating in his being seeming opposites and even contradictory qualities. He is not a patriarchal or matriarchal figure separate from mankind that one prays to in order to be in his or her favor. He is not a savior or redeemer—fundamentally, at most times, Shiva does not care. Shiva is pure consciousness, and united with Shakti, points to primal undivided being (see color plate 4).

And yet often some of these aspects of Shiva are forgotten, ignored, or distorted, even by the followers in his native lands. His essentially wild nature is tamed, the fierceness of his being downplayed. The blatantly obvious and often sexual symbolism surrounding him is distorted in favor of a more prudish "interpretation," which is a sign of the corruption of the times. Even the Shiva lingam and yoni are reduced to some kind of abstract symbols, when it is obvious what they represent. But the powerful eternal truths expressed in symbolic language are still there, present and intact for anyone to read (see color plate 5).

My journey was a journey in the patronage of Shiva, reflecting each man's journey to the soul's true homeland. A journey ascending to the highest peaks and descending to the lowest depths and experiencing and integrating both into one and the same being. This was yatra, pilgrimage.

Pilgrimage is to purposefully, intentionally give oneself to experience and momentarily shed one's attachments to one's familiar world and to enter another where the old rules do not necessarily apply. Perhaps it is only by striving for the lands of primal knowledge incarnate, which simultaneously mirror our own inner depths, that we can truly reach the shores of timeless truth. Perhaps this is the eternal quest of the hero, retold again and again in myth, legend, and story. And perhaps in a world with fewer and fewer heroes and fewer and fewer treasures worthy of a quest, this is what is important: to find the magic mirrors worth striving for—mirrors that reflect our own true nature and an undiluted truth.

# 2

# BETWEEN WORLDS

DAWN WAS BREAKING in downtown Mumbai, and we were bouncing around in the backseat of a taxi driving madly through the early morning traffic. My partner and I were on our way to Goa, but we still had a few hours before our plane would take off and so were headed for a quick visit to Chowpatty Beach, the major site of the yearly Ganesh Chaturthi festival (birthday of Lord Ganesh). Ganesh, son of Shiva and Parvati, is the lord of obstacles and new beginnings, who presides over wisdom, prosperity, and good fortune. This elephant-headed deity is one of the most popular and loved gods of all India and without question the patron god of Mumbai. As Ganesh is always invoked first in any puja or before any new undertaking, I thought it wise to start our new journey in India with an offering to him.

The Ganesh Chaturthi festival culminates in massive, elaborately constructed, painted, and decorated statues of the god being paraded into the sea. As with so many things in India, here too lies a curious paradox: the materials used to commercially manufacture the statues and the chemicals used to paint them pose a serious environmental problem for the waters, and the day after the immersion of the statues, massive amounts of dead fish can be seen floating on the surface of the sea.

It was surprisingly quiet when we arrived on Chowpatty Beach, with few people about, save for some families who lived there under the palm trees and the occasional child or dog strolling by, all equally perplexed to see white people there this early in the morning. The water was brownish, and the shoreline was literally filled to the brim with garbage, broken pottery, and the occasional brightly colored Ganesh statue. Still, several fishermen were silently spreading their nets in the waters. I had brought along a little clay icon of the big-bellied, elephant-headed god that I had found on my last journey to offer to the sea here so that he would protect our journey at its beginning and remove all obstacles that might arise. Thrice I silently spoke the Ganesh mantra before offering the statue for the sea to swallow.

In the taxi on the way back to the airport I felt like life was straight out of a film or comic book—life as fiction. It seemed as though in India everything operated according to some strange, magical logic and narrative, quite different from the way things are perceived in the modern secular world. Here, where rituals are part and parcel of daily life for most people and where there are altars everywhere, even on highways for drivers to flip coins at while driving by, it seemed like the most logical thing in the world to take a long taxi ride in an exhausted state in order to throw a little statue into the water, simply to obtain the blessings of an elephant-headed god. If nothing else, it seemed like a poetic act.

When we finally arrived in Goa, we went first to Anjuna Beach, a hippie-hangout remnant of the 1960s, and got a room with a balcony close to the shore. There we sat and had a drink in the shade of palm trees and listened to the waves of the Arabian Sea crashing ashore. Coming from the deep dark winter of the north, the sun was godly in its brilliance and seemed to light up our sooty spirits, as we stood with our bare feet in the sea and sand. In the morning, armies of crows would wake us up, and at night, the sound of waves would put us to sleep.

Equally, some aspects of Goa remained less paradisiacal. The pushy hecklers, merchants, and beggars were all there, waiting for us. As we walked by stalls selling statues, T-shirts, and psychedelically colored bric-a-brac, shadowy figures would emerge and recite the menu of dodgy drugs that were available. Even though many psychedelic plants are rooted in tradition and widely used all throughout India, the mere possession of something as innocent as cannabis might land you in jail for ten years—minimum—and the police were known to often be corrupt and plant drugs on hapless tourists for extortion.

It has been said repeatedly over the ages that magic manifests as an increase in meaningful signs and synchronicities, in seeming coincidences. It has also been said that should one desire a guide along the path, one will appear when the will is strong enough. I sought not theories and ideologies, but a living link to a living tradition of knowledge; I wanted not only to see the sadhus, magicians, and shamans, but I wanted to be able to see *as they saw*. This had, through a series of synchronicities, finally put me in contact with a real Naga Baba and a very rare one at that—he had Western roots and a command of the English language. I have also never been satisfied with mere images but have sought direct personal contact, and so there we were, on our way to his house in a taxi.

I did not really know what to expect—a wild madman garbed in ashes, a mild-mannered sadhu in ochre robes,* a shaman or a sham man, or all of these things rolled into one. When the taxi driver overheard me talking on the phone with Baba to ask for directions, he became visibly excited. As we arrived the taxi driver slammed on the brakes, forgot to ask us for payment (which never happens in India), and leapt out of the car, hoping for a chance to talk to—and perhaps

---

*Sadhus wear ochre because it is the color of fire. Also, in India, ochre is literally the color of earth, which marks the sadhus connection with the "Great Mother."

receive a blessing from—the man waiting for us outside his house. This epitomized how, even in this day and age, Babas still command primal respect and awe.

My initial trepidation vanished as we shook hands with this smiling, bearded older man called Baba Rampuri. We entered the Portuguese-style house and were guided into the living room, the walls of which were lined with pictures of various gurus whom I recognized as being from Rampuri's lineage. There were statues, Shiva lingams, and ritual items that formed altars on shelves and tables, as well as a substantial library and oriental carpets on the floor. At one of the main altars I immediately noted two long rare spiral horns (in the Himalayas they are used as trumpets by the traditional shamans*), which exactly mirrored ones I had tattooed as hidden talismans on myself.

The story goes that Rampuri is an American expatriate and the son of a surgeon, who left his home in California in the late 1960s at the age of nineteen to travel to India, where he eventually made his life. After traveling across the land, he met a rare English-speaking guru, Hari Puri Baba, and in one quick, life-defining moment became a *chela,* a disciple. He was given the name Rampuri and received the *panch guru* initiation, "the sacrament of the five gurus," losing his former self and life and simultaneously gaining a new one, becoming the first foreigner ever to be initiated into India's most ancient order of yogis and shamans, the Naga Sannyasis, or Naga Babas. His new name reflected the lineage of Babas of Juna Akhara, the ancient order of the Renunciates of the Ten Names. Despite all the adversity and strife he encountered as an outsider and foreigner, he received from his gurus the tradition of knowledge, often in the form of stories passed down from guru to disciple for thousands of years. This mystical tradition included sacred speech, mantras (magical formulae), tantra (philosophy and practice centered around the interaction between Shiva and Shakti, subject and

---

*Müller-Ebeling, Rätsch, and Shahi, *Shamanism and Tantra in the Himalayas.*

object, consciousness and energy/matter), ayurveda (a system of traditional medicine), astrology, logic, and ritual—all of which constitute the ancient tradition of yoga. Rampuri later founded the Hari Puri Ashram in the town of Hardwar at the foothills of the Himalayas, and has since become a high-ranking member in the hierarchy of his order of yogis, a member of the Council of Elders of Datt Akhara, Ujjain. Reflecting his very unlikely life story, he has written a book,* which gives a rare glimpse into the world of the Naga Babas.

We sat down on the sofa and his companion Adi Rana Puri, a young German woman, made us some tea as we started talking. Rampuri was a storyteller first and foremost, not interested in proselytization or dogma, nor in forcing any beliefs on us, or anyone else for that matter. He was "a local guy, not a universalist." Like a grandfather or a bard from a different age, he would weave us into his web of story that he himself had learned from his gurus, reflecting on some aspect of his tradition, while immersed in a smoke cloud of charas.

Rampuri's initial teachings came not in the form of abstract lessons but in conjunction with very real and concrete things of the world, such as food. My partner had problems with her stomach, so Rampuri gave her some herbal medicines and recommendations on what to eat and what to avoid. At the same time he gave a teaching of the *gunas,* the three qualities or tendencies of Prakriti, of all nature. As students of yoga, ayurveda, or of some aspect of the Indian esoteric tradition will know, the gunas consist of *rajas* (the active tendency), *tamas* (the passive tendency) and *sattva* (the balanced tendency). They are found in all of creation, in the five great elements of ether, air, fire, water, and earth.

Surely there was nothing for sale here—no ideologies, religions, tricks, or quick fixes. What Rampuri seemed to say was, "Give it all up."

When speaking of what relevance Rampuri's experience and

---

*Rampuri, *Autobiography of a Sadhu: A Journey into Mystic India* (Rochester, Vt.: Inner Traditions, 2010).

Fig. 2.1. Rampuri, Goa, India
(Photograph by the author)

knowledge has for European people and their lives, he said: "If one's purpose is the acquisition of knowledge, the acquisition of balance, then it's not important to become a good little Indian, it's not important to do what I have done, to think what I think, to live in a cave, to renounce the world—all of these things are superfluous. These things are those cultural elements that have allowed me to go deeper into an Indian tradition, but I don't think this is important for Western people, and I make a very strong point of saying this. I think the important thing for Western people interested in this area is that they have to get in touch with themselves. They have to get in touch with the spirits and deities of their own land, of their own sacred river goddesses, of the spirits of the forest, of the spirits of the sky, their blood, the soil underneath their feet . . . .

"If we had living traditions in the West, if we had living masters, teachers, and gurus who were part of a tradition in the sense that they were passing down what has been passed down to them and passed down to those before them, then I don't think that I would really even have much to say in the West. But the situation is that we don't. So it's my interest that I hold up a mirror to you, and you see yourself, and you see what lies behind you from a different view—but you are looking at yourself, and you are looking at your land and your culture. . . .

"And the answer is in the key to hermeticism which is analogy, that my experience in a living oral tradition can be a mirror that reflects one's soil and blood, in another way, an analogous reflection that points toward subtle or unseen aspects of their own lives and locality."

Analogy, therefore, seemed truly to be the key to an understanding of any of this.

When I talked about similarities between signs, such as the Algiz rune (ᛉ), the trident, and the trishul of Shiva, and how they seemed to signify similar things, Rampuri took out a statue of a horned figure and said, "This is the original trishul." The statue was based on a figure found in the Mohenjo-daro, one of the largest and oldest city

Fig. 2.2. Trishul over Varanasi
(Photograph by A. Haapapuro)

settlements (dating back to more than 2600 BCE, depending on the source) that depicts a figure with three faces, sitting cross-legged with bull-like horns, his whole head obviously resembling a trishul. This cross-legged horned figure bore a striking resemblance to various other horned gods (e.g., Dionysus, Bacchus, Pan, and Cernunnos) as well as to the archetypal image of the yogi and of Shiva himself.

Rampuri continued: "You see, there is a basic issue here that is very important when you are dealing with magic. The basic issue is: Are you using something that is a sign, or something that is a symbol? Are you using something that is marking something of the world, or are you using something that is referencing an idea? Now, ideas are fickle, and ideas change during the course of time and over geography. So I think that if we are using symbols, which Carl Jung was so fond of and wanted to attribute some sort of universalism to, I think we get stuck in a particular time and place. In magic, we are looking for things that don't mark the fickle ideas of man, but mark things of the world that we can see reflected in different ways: we can see reflected in the night sky, in the stars, we can see reflected in the topography of the planet, in the mountains, rivers, and deserts, we can see reflected in the animal world, we can see reflected in plants, we can see reflected in our faces, our eyes, nose, and our physical structure. This is the direction I believe we have to go in if we are maintaining the discourse of magic, rather than the discourse of modern Western philosophy and psychology. So, when we look at something like horns or a trishul, and we say that the trishul marks the three gunas, or Brahma-Vishnu-Shiva—yes, it's OK for discussion, for entertainment and so forth, but I don't think it gets us into this other space, which is a reflected space, which is a revealed space. The key here is a word that was used again and again in European hermeticism, that Paracelsus, for example, was very fond of, and the word is *resemblance*. Resemblance says to us: when something resembles something else, it is a mark that indicates hidden relationships, relationships that exist below the surface."

On the significance of synchronicities, Rampuri said: "Where you have a resemblance, this is not a statement in itself, this is not a symbol in the sense that we immediately start the interpretation. This is not the treasure; this is the mark. On the surface of the world—not the surface of the Earth, but the surface of the world—we see a mark, we see a big *X*, and it says to us: 'Dig here.' This is the significance to me."

I told Rampuri I liked his personal story because he was, in the beginning at least, an outsider. And as a born outsider myself, I could relate to this, not just in the sense of being the outsider but also in the sense of a "spiritual" outsider like Shiva. Rampuri interrupted me, exclaiming: "Shiva, the ultimate outsider!

"You said that I have been the outsider and that I have become an insider. I would disagree with that. I started out as an outsider, and now I am even more an outsider. A lot of this, of course, is based on circumstance: I am part of an Indian esoteric tradition, but I am a foreigner, and the fact of my foreign birth will always keep me an outsider in the Indian esoteric tradition. And yet, because I am so much a part of the Indian esoteric tradition, it prevents me from ever being an insider in any other tradition. I make a remark in my book when I realize that I am possessed, that I am even an outsider among outsiders. I think it's the outsider that has the ability, or at least has the opportunity, to look at things from a distance, rather than being in the midst of things and assigning some sort of moral values, the good and bad, the good and evil, to things. So I think that many, if not most, people who have insights, who have particular geniuses in various fields, whether it's music or art or literature or whatever—I think that a requirement is that one is an outsider."

After talking for several hours, we had dinner in a restaurant and lassis in a little juice shop. I was strangely affected by the meeting, feeling both stimulated and disquieted at the same time.

In India, many discussions inevitably lead to religion, magic, and spirituality—*spirituality,* a word that always made me cringe in discomfort. "Are you a Hindu?" I was asked many times. Raj, the young man working at the place where we stayed, enthusiastically explained that he was a "Vishnu kind of guy." "Vishnu is the god for the common man," he said. One day Raj brought me a little note on which he had written the popular Gayatri mantra, which he thought I might find beneficial. Later still, he even bought me a gift. It was a book, or rather a booklet, by a wacked-out, starry-eyed Western guy, a Goan regular. On the back cover it said: "You shine without a shadow. Follow the light, and you will never get lost. Let love guide your way, and you shall find peace unto your soul." In the booklet he wrote about angels looking out for him over his shoulder, even when things took a turn for the worse . . . such as when his friend lost his dentures in the sea.

It all seemed hopelessly out of balance, disconnected from the stark realities of life, epitomizing something sadly comical about how spirituality tends to manifest in general: rather than an enhancement of reality, it is an escape from it.

In a Shaivite temple we visited, the usual commotion was going on in front of the altar where the white-clad pandits were accepting offerings and giving out blessings. When I brought forth my offering, a pandit suddenly approached me and shouted, "From which country?" to which I replied, "Finland." Without blinking, he said, "Aah, Jumala Shiva!" (meaning "God Shiva" in Finnish). I was not quite sure what to make of this sudden breaking of the language barrier that one normally encountered from vendors selling souvenirs at tourist hot spots. I received some vibhuti on my third eye and a red and orange thread on my right wrist.

But on a deeper level, the doors of the temples remained closed to those from outside of this world and its language. I remained a tourist—and perhaps it was for the better. To penetrate the veil in a deeper sense would require a lifetime of effort and dedication. I was and would ever remain an outsider in this world, parts of which I felt a connection to, and other parts that I felt instinctively repelled by. Not being knowledgeable in either Hindi or Sanskrit, except for some rudimentary basics, and being a foreigner, I was a *mleccha*, a barbarian and an outcast, and despite whatever affinities I had, they would not change this fact.

We moved from Anjuna to Arambol Beach and into a little bamboo shack high on a steep hill overlooking the ocean. At night we would listen to the waves as they roared below. At dawn and dusk, I would sometimes hear the distant ringing of bells coming from somewhere above, mingling with the sound of the waves. I asked about it and was told that there was a little outdoor temple on the top of the hill precisely above our hut, but even the locals didn't seem to know much more than that.

One morning, my partner and I woke up in our little bamboo shack on the hill and felt like shit. Some days just seem intrinsically bad, in a deep, troubling way. If I were versed in Indian astrology I could tell you that it was due to this or that negative planetary influence. But be that as it may, this was definitely one of those days. I looked over the seashore and wondered why it was so quiet down there on the beach. A little later we were violently vomiting and shitting our insides out, dazed in a fever. During the day we began receiving text messages from friends and family asking us if we were all right. Apparently there had been some kind of terrorist attack somewhere in India.

The next day, still weary from the sickness, I wandered down to the bar to get some water and look at the newspapers. In capital letters the panicked headlines screamed: MUMBAI TERRORIST ATTACKS. A group of young men had attacked several major hotels and tourist hot spots in Mumbai with AK-47s and hand grenades. They targeted Indians and whites, specifically Britons and Americans, but in effect this meant all Western-looking people. A picture of a fiery-eyed twenty-year-old man in a T-shirt wielding a Kalashnikov assault rifle leered from the front page. I felt another wave of nausea building up.

The same young man was later captured at a popular evening destination for locals and the main site for the annual celebrations of Ganesh Chaturthi, Chowpatty Beach—coincidentally the same place we had visited only a few days earlier. They had also had a shooting spree right beside the place where we were supposed to travel to in just a day or two. The newspapers featured pictures and descriptions of the "pools of blood." The siege was still going on, and tourists were advised to avoid train stations and airports. There were also police boats guarding the coastlines of India, especially those areas frequented by tourists.*

All of this made us feel rather gloomy, and an ominous feeling crept over what was supposed to be a recharging experience. The beaches were unusually silent and an underlying tension was in the air. "Don't worry," the ever-optimistic Raj told me, "such things always happen in India." And come to think of it, they do. In all of my travels in India, I have always just barely missed being at the site of a bombing or conflagration. Perhaps Ganesh has been looking out for me after all.

Drawn by the sound of the bells again ringing from somewhere above our shack, I finally walked to the top of the hill at dusk. I discovered it was a little shrine to Guru Dattatreya, the lord of yogis and the messenger of the gods. Guru Dattatreya is the primordial yogi, the original or "first teacher," bringer of knowledge and giver of initiation. He is characterized by his three heads (those of Brahma, Vishnu, and Shiva: creator, sustainer, and destroyer), is often shown naked with long, matted locks that merge with the earth, and is accompanied by a cow and

---

*These were the 2008 Mumbai terrorist attacks, which killed 164 people and wounded at least 308.

four dogs. He is the one who is called upon to give teachings and initiation, while the other earthly gurus stand by as witness gurus presiding over this process. Dattatreya is the patron of all Naga Babas—including Rampuri. And of all the bamboo huts in Goa, I had chosen this one, directly under Dattatreya's shrine on the hilltop.

I spoke to Rampuri over the phone and told him we were feeling weary from the sickness and low in spirits. He told us to come over as he could help us with traditional medicine and a healing puja. When we arrived, we talked about terrorism as a sign of the Kali Yuga, the fourth and last age in the cycle of ages, characterized by strife and degeneration. Rampuri gave us some Ayurvedic medicine, and we began the evening puja. As Rampuri and Adi Rana Puri lighted and waved some ghee (clarified butter) at one of the altars, they started intoning one of the traditionally most powerful mantras, the great death-conquering Mahamrityunjaya mantra:

ॐ त्र्यम्बकं यजामहे
सुगन्धिं पुष्टिवर्धनम्
उर्वारुकमिव बन्धनान्
मृत्योर्मुक्षीय मामृतात्

*Om Tryambakam yajāmahe*
*sugandhim pushti vardhanam,*
*urvārukamiva bandhanān*
*mrityormokshiya māmritām.**

_____

*English translation: "Om—We worship the Three-Eyed Lord who is fragrant and who nourishes and nurtures all beings. As the ripened cucumber is freed from the bondage of its creeper, may He liberate us from death for the sake of immortality." The difficulty in translating mantras is that in the Indian esoteric tradition, the mantras do not only refer to spoken language and sound, but to sacred speech and *place*. Mantras consist of a river of sacred syllables that mark places on Earth and in the dome of the sky, and likewise, in the dome of the mouth. These mirror each other as the hermetic axiom, and together they form the great story, the great chain of resemblances, which is upheld by the esoteric tradition.

We went around the house as he rang the bell and waved burning ghee lamps above various pictures and statues, starting with a large statue of Ganesh. "Ganesh is the Lord of Obstacles, so we always invoke him first." The puja was conducted at one of the altars, with the traditional blowing of the conch-shell trumpet and the recitation of mantras and singing of *bhajans,* devotional songs to Shiva and the gods. He offered us sacred water and *prasad,* "that which pleases," a sweet food that is first offered to the gods and then, when the gods are pleased, distributed among the devotees. Lastly, he gave us Rudraksha seeds to wear on our necks as malas.

The Rudraksha is the seed of the Rudraksha tree, sacred to and named after a form of Shiva. In India many stories are told about the Rudraksha, and a whole magical and medicinal art has sprung up around it. The story goes that Rudra—who is the wildest, fiercest, and least compassionate form of Shiva—was high above the world of ordinary men in his celestial abode in the mountains, immersed in deep meditation ("He doesn't give a fuck," in Rampuri's words). One day he opened his eyes and descended down to the world of men, whom he saw hopelessly locked in ignorance, stupidity, and suffering. The sight moved him to such a degree that he, Rudra, the fierce, wild, uncompassionate one, shed tears for what he saw. Where his tears fell, there grew the Rudraksha tree with its dark red seeds. Since then the Rudraksha seeds, the eyes or tears of Shiva (*āksa* means "eye," hence "Rudra eyes") are thought to mark knowledge and health. They are Shiva's gift to man to aid him in overcoming the stupidity and ignorance that lead to suffering. Those dedicated to Shiva have worn the seeds as signs of their dedication to him, and they are a mark of discipleship.

Before the puja, Rampuri had said I would feel better afterward, and I did. While having our last dinner together at a restaurant named—in typical Goan fashion—Bean Me Up, Rampuri told us about his experiences when he first entered the Naga Babas. He

Fig. 2.3. Hilltop shrine to Dattatreya, the three-headed messenger
of the gods and tantric lord of yogis
(Photograph by the author)

had been expecting to practice *asanas* (yogic postures) and mantras, to delve into a magical world and a rigorous esoteric routine. Instead he spent a lot of time cleaning pots and pans, providing simple service to his gurus and the dhuni, and essentially taking care of cooking and cleaning. While talking about spirituality and the hollowness of that word, Rampuri ended by saying: "At the end of the day, there is no spirituality." Then he paused. "Because you have to make dinner?" I asked. "Because you have to make dinner," he replied with a little smile.

Our last day in India began with a sunrise puja and ended with a sunset puja at the hilltop shrine to Dattatreya, the messenger of the gods. I bought some offerings and incense to lay at the altar (see color plate 6) and rang the bells hanging on the trees. Standing at the edge of the cliff, watching a giant bird hover in the air, the scorching sun above and the roaring sea below, I realized I was at an edge of worlds in more ways than one. And as Rampuri would say, that's where the magic happens.

# 3
# INITIATION

IT WAS THE HEIGHT OF SUMMER, and I found myself deep in a lush forest adjacent to a lake and river in the countryside of Sweden—practically in the middle of nowhere. I had made pilgrimage to this remote place that was to be a *tirtha,* a crossing-over place, where the ordinary and extraordinary worlds meet. Surrounded by trees and water, a dhuni had been constructed to serve as the focal point of invocation. This was to be a place of acquiring knowledge in the traditional way, orally, and via participation, revelation, and invocation.

The very small retreat was organized by two young and beautiful hatha yoga teachers, Savitri Puri from Sweden and Yogananda Puri from Denmark, and consisted of two handfuls of people from different European countries, careers, and backgrounds. Sacred speech, which forms the foundation of the esoteric tradition of yoga, mantra, tantra, ayurveda, and astrology, was to be the focus of the retreat. This knowledge does not come in the form of a text or a book but a living oral tradition, resting on the authority of the tradition itself, passed down through the ages from teacher to disciple. Rampuri was such an authority, and an extremely rare one at that because of his Western background. He was a link to a living esoteric tradition, a foot in the door to a world that would otherwise be totally off-limits.

*Havan,* the ancient Vedic fire ritual, marked the beginning of the week-long delving into magic, invocation, and sacred speech. Rampuri, who had traveled from India to Sweden to host the retreat, rang the bell outside the little yurt that had been raised in the forest surrounding the dhuni and with a forceful blow smashed a coconut on a stone on the ground outside of it. The dhuni, which had been extensively decorated with rice, flowers, colored powders, and symmetrical, geometric symbols called *yantras* (seats for the deities), was ceremonially lighted. Agni, the fire god, was called upon, along with all the other deities and spirits of earth, water, air, and ether. In this ornate and elaborate ritual, the fire was fed with offerings, sacrifices, and sacred substances such as incense, herbal mixtures, and ghee, along with recitals of mantras punctuated by the chanting of "Svaha," the name of Agni's wife. Water from the Ganga, Yamuna, and several European rivers was sprinkled in all directions. And all the gods, spirits, and plant deities were invoked to be with us there for that time and give their blessings of knowledge, health, and prosperity.

Each morning I woke up and bathed in the clear lake right beside the dhuni, and every night I fell asleep to the sound of the adjacent river. In the morning at sunrise and evening at sunset an aarti puja was performed. Those twilight moments between worlds were the favorite times of Shiva. Preceding each puja, the altar was decorated with fresh flowers, plants, and substances, and likewise at the conclusion of each puja, everyone was offered sacred fire, as well as water, vibhuti, and prasad to eat. Bhajans were sung. The pujas were anything but quiet meditations: bells rang, conch-shell trumpets pierced the air, horns blared, and cymbals and gongs clashed in loud invocations, as the air filled with smoke and sound.

Rampuri gave *satsang,* teachings, revolving around the revelation of what he called "sacred speech" within everyone present, identifying speech as place rather than sound. We carefully identified each one of the indestructible syllables that form the core of sacred speech, called *matrikas,* or "little mothers," that together form the great chain of resemblances, the totality of speech and knowledge—the "Great Mother."

What Rampuri taught was completely different from the yoga we think of in the West. It was not about "feeling good," not about holding hands and chanting Om, not about some kind of exercise system where you stand on your head, and there was not a New Ager in sight. It was also not about belief systems or wacky ideas that seem so popular these days but about knowledge that required intelligence and discipline. Yoga, as taught in the traditional way, was more akin to European magic and alchemy than to anything normally associated with it. Even its figurehead, Guru Dattatreya, also called Avadhut (messenger of the gods), who has three heads (those of the creator, preserver, and destroyer), bore a resemblance to Hermes (messenger of the gods) Trismegistus (thrice great).

The French historian and Shaivite Alain Daniélou alludes in his works to a primordial tradition and religion at the root of humanity, a kind of Ur religion from whence sprang several traditions mirroring the original, of which the traditions of Shiva and Dionysus are primary examples. He wrote: "This early religion is the outcome of man's efforts since his remotest origins to understand the nature of creation in its balanced beauty and cruelty, as well as the manner in which he can identify himself in the Creator's work and cooperate with him. This religion is naturistic, not moralistic, ecstatic and not ritualistic."*

In contrast to the moralistic religions and arbitrary ideologies of modern societies, Daniélou suggested that this Shaivite/Dionysian primordial religion expressed more direct, more instinctually pure ways of communication with the creative forces of life. As its figureheads stood archetypal figures such as Dionysus, Shiva, and similar gods from other ancestral pantheons and cultures.

---

*Daniélou, *Gods of Love and Ecstasy,* 7.

Whereas the living bacchanalian cults and traditions of Dionysian figures have been largely forgotten in the West and lie dormant in culture, custom, mythology, and symbolism, a tradition of Shiva was still alive in India. I was anxious to make a connection to such a living tradition that somehow managed to exist in the modern world. "Yes, Shiva, Dionysus, Pan, and don't forget the Dark Mother, whether Kali, Loralei, or some of yours," said Rampuri.

But Shiva and the Indian gods were not the only ones invoked. All the local gods, the spirits of the place, as well as the ancestral gods that the people present carried within themselves in their blood, were invoked as well. For the concluding havan of the retreat Rampuri asked me to compile a specific, detailed list of the major gods from different pantheons and cultures represented here by distinct individuals. This reflected something characteristic of India and indeed of its nondualistic traditions: that there is only One, but the One—in reflection of its own boundless, immense nature—takes on infinite manifestations and forms.

After revealing the matrikas to us, it was time for the concluding havan and the initiation for those who desired it. A few people would receive new names according to the tradition. These new names would function as talismans and establish a living connection to the tradition as well as a particular family of Babas. The name is decided on by the Baba, based on the character, given name, and birth star of the person receiving it. My birth star happened to be Punarvasu, the same as Rampuri's.

On the day of initiation, I took a long, final bath in the lake under the scorching sun. I swam for a lotus flower growing on the surface of the water, which I was to give to Rampuri at my initiation. As I watched my reflection on the still surface of the lake, I thought of Rampuri's words: "When Shiva looks in the mirror, he sees Shakti."

A red-and-yellow cord was tied around my right wrist. I entered the enclosure, where Rampuri was expecting me, along with Yogananda

Fig. 3.1. When Shiva looks in the mirror, he sees Shakti. Tirtha,
a sacred crossing-over place in rural Sweden.
(Photograph by the author)

Puri, who acted as a witness to the proceedings. I paid my respects to the dhuni and to the Baba presiding over it, as is the tradition, and presented him with the lotus flower, as well as a small sum in coins that were put in a *kapala* (human skull bowl).

Three times I asked to receive initiation. Thereafter Rampuri pointed to the decorated, three-headed Dattatreya statue at the dhuni and said:

"Now you have asked three times for initiation and you shall receive it. Dattatreya, the naked one, the lord of all yogis, is the one who grants initiation, the one who shows the path, as I am merely a witness guru."

Rampuri called upon the sacred fire, the gods and spirits, as witnesses to the initiation. He smashed a coconut in half with a violent blow, and the broken shell flowed with milk. He took my head close to his and whispered in my ear. From the silence the mantra came as a whirlwind, thrice, syllable after syllable, connected to each other with a bindu in a great chain. This was the *varna mala,* Kali's garland of fifty-one skulls, mirroring the fifty-one syllables of the Sanskrit alphabet, the totality of speech and knowledge.

I was given the name Adinath Puri. Puri is the name of the lineage, the family, whereas Adinath, or Adi Nath, or even Adi Natha, as previously mentioned, means "First Lord," the progenitor of all yogis and shamans, that is, a name for Shiva, pure consciousness and ultimate reality. "A very strong, powerful name that you can grow into," said Rampuri with a smile, while putting a Rudraksha around my neck and giving me water, vibhuti, and prasad to eat.

Afterward, I felt strange, overwhelmed, and otherworldly, like I walked just a little bit above the ground. I had just been given a mantra and a new name and made a living connection and relationship to an age-old lineage and tradition of knowledge. Not really being able to communicate this to others, I took a long walk in the woods. Later on, I went and asked Rampuri about this unexpected feeling, and he assured me that the common reaction to initiation is total confusion.

Fig. 3.2. The dhuni and the Baba presiding over it
(Photograph by the author)

He told me a story about his own experience of it when he was young. Apparently, just prior to the initiation, the reluctant and apprehensive Rampuri had asked his Baba, "Am I ready for this?" to which the old Baba answered, "You are never ready for this!"

We laughed. With my spirits uplifted, I took my leave.

As I returned to the ordinary world and watched the changing vistas from the window of the train, I felt lighter. One of the last things said by Rampuri before I left rang in my ears: "And if nothing else, you have learned how to drink water by the drop and eat ashes."

# 4

# KUMBH MELA— THE LAST RITES

IT WAS THE FOLLOWING SPRING, a half year after my initiation, and I was on a train again, headed for the Kumbh Mela, the largest gathering of people for a spiritual, magical, or religious purpose on planet Earth. The train was packed to the hilt, and it was a small miracle that I had been able to secure a ticket the evening before. Unpleasantly hot even in the middle of the night, the train filled with sounds of rattling, snoring, and farting. I was on my way from Delhi via the night train to Hardwar, a journey of only a little over 120 miles, which nevertheless took virtually all night. As I lay awake in the uppermost bunk bed of three in the shuffling train compartment, having arrived in India the previous morning, I sensed something different from my past journeys here. Sometimes all the things one gathers and carries along with oneself can become a heavy load to bear. Perhaps this time I was here to let go of something, to cleanse myself of something.

As the train finally arrived, the bustling city of Hardwar looked surreal in the early morning twilight. Everywhere there were people, so many of them, and I had to step over sleeping bodies scattered on the ground to get anywhere. People from all over India, as well as from everywhere else in the world, kept arriving here in droves, train upon train, busload after busload, by vehicle or on foot. The roads were regularly closed to public traffic, which meant that you could not get into the city at all. Everywhere there were families, beggars, pilgrims, soldiers, and especially sadhus of all kinds. In the past sadhus were a relatively rare sight for me to behold, but now suddenly they were everywhere. They sat under trees and stared, with that haunting, otherworldly look that is characteristic of them. But all of this was not really a surprise. The Kumbh Mela was after all a gathering of such magnitude that it was actually visible from space. And I, at heart a loner, who often felt crowded even in just a room full of people, was now here in the midst of this raging, swarming mass of millions.

The city of Hardwar is situated at the foothills of the Himalayas. From the high mountains the river Ganga runs through it, wide and strong. A giant figure of Shiva, visible from miles away, guards the city at its entrance. Indeed, the city is considered a gateway to Shiva and the gods, and its name derives from Har or Hara, a name of Shiva, and *dwar,* meaning door. Its other names reflect this as well: Haridwar, (the gateway of the sustaining god, Vishnu, also called Hari), Gangadwar (the gateway of the Ganga), Brahmadwar (the gateway of Brahma, the god of creation), and Mayadwar (the door of illusion, Maya), which is said to be its most ancient name. Statues, temples, shrines, and signs of Shiva and the gods were everywhere, and indeed the whole city itself seemed to be one gigantic altar between worlds. There was never a moment of silence, as from the early hours to late evening the bhajans and pujas resounded across the shores of the river.

I arrived at my destination by the Ganga at dawn and had chai while looking over the massive river, ever flowing with offerings of flowers, coconuts, and pieces of cloth, as monkeys fished the waters for edible stuff. On the other side of the river, sadhus and pilgrims wandered and took baths along the banks, and behind them multitudes of tents were set up. As the sun rose from behind the mountains in an orange halo, bells and songs echoed across the shore. Everyone was here for this river, and everything happened in close conjunction with it.

The origins of the Kumbh Mela festival are steeped in ancient history, going back to mythological events. Kumbh Mela is a composite of two words: *kumbh* from Sanskrit, meaning "pitcher" (as for carrying water), and *mela* meaning "fair" or "gathering." The story goes that the gods and demons came together to churn the primordial ocean of milk for the greatest of treasures, *amrit,* the nectar of immortality, to be distributed to everyone afterward. However, one of the demons sneaked in line and stole the pitcher containing the amrit. For twelve days and nights (equal to twelve human years) the gods and demons fought over the pitcher. At one point Krishna flew away with the pot, accidentally spilling four drops from it that landed on the Earth. Those four places are now among the holiest in all of India—Prayag, Hardwar, Ujjain, and Nashik—and are the sites of the Kumbh Mela held every four years. At specific dates and times in these places, according to the position of the sun, moon, and stars, it is said that amrit appears. And on those dates everyone comes here to take a bath in the Ganga and to receive a drop of the amrit; millions and millions of people become pilgrims for those brief moments when the heavenly, death-conquering nectar is flowing, echoing a tradition from time immemorial.

In his travelogue *Following the Equator,* Mark Twain wrote of the Kumbh:

It is wonderful, the power of a faith like that, that can make multitudes upon multitudes of the old and weak and the young and frail enter without hesitation or complaint upon such incredible journeys and endure the resultant miseries without repining. It is done in love, or it is done in fear; I do not know which it is. No matter what the impulse is, the act born of it is beyond imagination, marvelous to our kind of people, the cold whites.*

Being a "cold white" myself, I had to agree with Twain. It was pretty marvelous, quite unlike anything I had ever seen. When I arrived at Hardwar, some of the major bathing days were approaching. There was a steady buzz going and one could feel an energy escalating. All of this, whatever *this* was, was gathering momentum like a rising storm.

At every moment pujas, rituals, and ceremonies were going on. At Har Ki Pauri, the ghats of the gods, there was a constant swarm of people pushing and shoving to take a bath in the Ganga, and every evening the spectacular Ganga aarti was conducted there. Equally crowded were the pilgrimage routes to the three temples—each dedicated to a different goddess—on the mountaintops surrounding Hardwar. The streets were filled with parades of one kind or another—some streets were closed even to pedestrians—and often it was literally impossible to walk in any other way than the crowds were moving. And all the time, more and more people kept arriving.

In the middle of this storm of activity, amid the crowds and the hustle and bustle, there was a center of relative calm (and I use the term *relative calm* in the loosest way possible)—the Juna Akhara. The Juna Akhara is the largest division of the mystical, militant order of Naga Babas, reputedly founded in the prehistoric Treta age by Dattatreya, the naked one. They were finally organized into a proper order by Adi Shankara in the fifth century BCE to protect Sanatan Dharma—the "Hindu" religion, but what the Naga Babas themselves view as the natural order of the universe. And they consider themselves to be the maintainers of the law of nature. This was also the order of which Baba Rampuri was a part.

---

*Mark Twain, *Following the Equator,* repr. ed. (Biblioteca Virtual Universal, 2008). Available online at http://www.biblioteca.org.ar/libros/167735.pdf.

Centered around the Maya Devi Temple, the temple of the goddess of illusion, the Juna Akhara was a sprawling encampment of a literal army of Naga Babas—the naked ones, the wild, wandering mystics, the holy madmen of Shiva. Their encampments consisted of shacks built around the multitudes of dhunis that were tended by an entourage of ghostly looking creatures. Stepping into the Akhara encampment was like stepping into another time and another world—an extraordinary world, where all previous rules and rationality simply ceased to exist. Instead it was a world of continuous invocation—of spirits, ghosts, freaks, and geezers, of wizards and creeps—a storybook world made flesh in the twenty-first century.

It was evening when I entered the Juna Akhara encampment for the first time. In my hand I had a book wrapped in a red and golden shroud, inside of which was my chosen *dakshina,* a traditional monetary gift to honor my patron. I approached the dhuni, surrounded by Rampuri's entourage of Naga Babas, removed my shoes, and clasped my hands together, saying "Om Namo Narayan" to all those present. "Om Namo Narayan!" came the booming chorus in response. I greeted, in the traditional way, first the dhuni and then the Babas presiding over it. The stern-looking Babas eyed me somewhat suspiciously as I paid my respects and received some water and ashes. I had also brought some flowers and after I set them decoratively at the sides of the dhuni, I sat down in silence. A few of the Babas finally nodded in smiling agreement.

My initial reaction to all of this, of course, as I told Rampuri a few days later, was a strong "What the fuck am I doing here?" It was all quite overwhelming and disorienting, suddenly bursting into this alien, foreign fairy-tale world. Rampuri said that it was good that I had told him. He continued, "What do I know—I've been sitting at the dhuni for the past forty years!"

Rampuri offered me an analogy for my situation. I was no longer my ordinary self, but a character, Adinath Puri, in a story written on the surface of the stars. The story was not a new one, but indeed the great story of all times: the story of the quest of the hero.

"It's like in *Star Wars* when Luke Skywalker first meets his teacher, Obi-Wan Kenobi, who tells him he has a destiny to fulfill. But Luke rejects it saying he must return home to his aunt to help with the cleaning, only to find that his home has been destroyed in his absence. It is the resistance of the call, and the next part of the story would be the conflict."

*Oh, great,* I thought. *A* Star Wars *analogy.*

Be that as it may, the dhuni of Rampuri was the place I made my center and focus during my stay in Hardwar, attending it daily after dawn and dusk. The dhuni, the sacred ritual fire that never went out and of which there were hundreds and hundreds, was the center of all attention. It was the temple, the altar, and the deity and was fed with offerings and mantras. Around the dhuni sits the Baba with his entourage and devotees, surrounded by pictures of gurus from times past, the whole scenario resembling a hall of mirrors stretching into infinity (see color plate 7).

The square of the dhuni was decorated daily with fresh flowers and purifying cow dung. It was sprinkled with water and given offerings of everything that was consumed by its side. It was always kept clean, and no rubbish was to ever be burned in its flames. A trishul raised skyward from its ashes, and a jug of water, a *kamandal,* rested at its rim. The fire is Agni, the fire god. The outer fire is in turn reflective of the inner fire, and at the dhuni, both are invoked. I was reminded of a line from the Mahābhārata: "Fire only exists by destroying the fuel which makes it live, by consuming the oblation. The whole universe, both sentient and insentient, is nothing but fire and oblation."

Each morning I wandered down the street, past the rows of lined-up beggars, over the bridge under which—among hordes of wild boars—a man was, like the animals, searching for valuables in the mountains of garbage, and past the ever-swelling crowds until finally I arrived at the gates of the Akhara and was waived in by the soldiers on guard there. Every time I arrived at the dhuni, I made sure I brought something pleasant, some sweet things to eat, some flowers, or a small dakshina.

Twice daily, around noon and late at night, the kitchen offered food to everyone. The "kitchen" was actually a shack in the corner of a makeshift tent, with extremely basic cooking utensils on an earthen floor. Despite these conditions, the Baba chefs managed to make some of what was truly the tastiest Indian food I have ever eaten. One would sit on a thin mat on the ground and be served as much delicious food as one wanted to eat, and all the while there was a stern-eyed Baba presiding over the meals, eating his own food from a skull-shaped bowl. At the recommendation of Rampuri, I had most of my meals there, and for the very first time during the course of all my travels in India, I remained healthy and free of stomachaches throughout my journey.

Tea and coffee, not to mention the charas, were also constantly being served. Consumption of meat and alcohol is forbidden in Hardwar, as it is considered a holy city and these things are traditionally taboo in the Hindu world. On the other hand charas is smoked in unimaginable quantities, literally by the truckloads, from morning to night every day for months on end. Luckily I had some whiskey with me, and I would sit late at night by the Ganga, listening to the echoing songs and invocations and discretely having a few drinks from a coffee cup. I was sure Shiva wouldn't mind—after all, he was often depicted in an inebriated state and was "the drinker of poisons."

Constant greeting shouts of "Om Namo Narayan!" heralded the arrival of someone at the dhuni. It is said that Shiva is accompanied by an entourage of ganas, whom Alain Daniélou described as follows:

In Shivaite tradition, the god's companions are described as a troupe of freakish, adventurous, delinquent, and wild young people, who prowl in the night, shouting in the storm, singing, dancing, and ceaselessly playing outrageous tricks on sages and gods. . . . The Ganas mock the rules of ethics and social order. They personify the joy of living, courage, and imagination, which are all youthful values. . . . These delinquents of heaven are always there to restore true values and to assist the "god-mad" who are persecuted and mocked by the powerful. They personify everything which is feared by and displeases bourgeois society, and which is contrary to the good morale of a well-policed city and its palliative concepts.*

When one looked at the regular crowd that attended the dhuni, their resemblance to the ganas was unmistakable. The Naga Babas were ash covered and sometimes completely naked. These long-haired, wild-eyed, strange and strong characters carried conch shells and musical instruments, trishuls, and swords or other weapons, signifying their status as warriors. Shouting invocations to Shiva, "Aalekh!" or "Bom!" they inhaled the thick smoke from the chillums filled with charas, which they smoked *all the time*. There was a constant chorus of wet coughing that went along with the nonstop chillum smoking. There were farts and burps, as well as the occasional instruments being played and songs being sung. Indeed at times, especially late in the evenings, nobody talked much, and most in attendance would just sit around stoned, their eyes half-closed, smiling that self-satisfied smile, looking like they were in possession of a some great secret. This was the divine stoner party of Shiva's holy madmen.

Sitting by the dhuni, I came to know some of these Babas. There was Mangalanand Puri (formerly Mangalanand Giri), also known as Goa Gil, a world-renowned guru of the Goa techno-trance dance scene. Most of the time sitting to the right of Rampuri, Mangalanand Puri was equipped with a constant, deep smile and an utterly disarming presence. Making chillums all the while, he would easily break

_____
*Daniélou, *Gods of Love and Ecstasy*, 99.

into laughter that seemed capable of breaking possible tensions and conflicts.

Early one morning, after I had been sitting at the dhuni for a few days, not really talking much to the Babas yet, Mangalanand Puri suddenly exclaimed to me, with his trademark joyfulness:

"Isn't it wonderful?!"

I nodded, and he continued:

"It's like when you go to the mountains, camping or trekking, and you lie there under the stars at night, when suddenly you have the realization of the cathedral of nature, the universe, god, the Cosmic Spirit, or whatever you choose to call it, and at that moment you understand how you and everything fits into that! We Babas choose to give up everything to live in that wondrous moment, in that Oneness of Life always, and that's why we don't have worldly ambitions, families, do work, or live the normal lives of the masses! We choose to remain in that realization and that life under the stars forever!" Then he punctuated the thought with his easy laughter.

There was Shakti Giri, a flamboyant, middle-aged Baba riding a flashy motorcycle plastered with various trishuls and swastikas, whom I became sort of friends with despite our convoluted conversations. With almost childlike enthusiasm he would take out his little box of treasures to show me his coin collection, to which I contributed a two-euro coin. He would say, "Double Shakti!" while pounding on his chest, and I'd say, "Triple Shakti," and he'd laugh. One day he examined the tattoos on my right arm closely and pointing to a tridentlike rune he asked, "Trishul?" I answered, "My homeland trishul," to which he said the oft-heard phrase pointing to an underlying resemblance: "Same, same." Going on to read the palm of my hand, he pointed at a line exclaiming, "Shiva!" and to another saying, "Long life, eighty years."

"Adinath Puri Ji!" I heard someone calling out on the street during my second or third day at the Mela. "Adinath Puri Ji, Rampuri is looking for you!" It was Surendra Puri, one of the rare Babas who spoke

English well. He was in his thirties, about my age, and had huge matted locks rolled up on top of his head and reaching all the way down to the ground, and a soft, warm but strong and disciplined presence. Like many Babas it seemed, he had been to military school before becoming a Baba. When I asked him something, his reply would be kind and welcoming. "Of course, Adinath Puri Ji. This your family, this your home." On one of the first days, he took me to the Maya Devi temple for darshan, and while we walked around the temple, he described the various manifestations of the Goddess.

There were also many Babas actively practicing tapasya of varying severities. Tapasya, physical and spiritual yogic austerities and mortifications that often involve severe vows, ordeals, or endurance of pain and suffering of a marked kind, are practiced to cultivate the inner fire (tapas) and to "get the attention of god." The motivation for the austerities lies not in the realms of guilt, sin, or repentance, as they would in a Christian context, but in the manipulation of matter for the cultivation of the spirit. Their nakedness is not indicative of some kind of sexuality but rather their renunciation of the ordinary world. Babas ideally use *kama,* the fire of passion and lust, as a source of tapas by burning it through austerities. They claim not to deny their sexuality, but to choose to control it, sublimate it, and retain it to transform it into spiritual or magical power.

As I understand it, practicing tapasya is a form of spiritual machismo, wherein the *tapasvin* (the practitioner), after going through some form of extreme austerity, such as climbing a mountain barefoot or living in an icy cave in the Himalayas, becomes untouchable, gaining a kind of divine power from the experience. There was the old Muni Baba, with gray-white matted locks and beard, who had taken a vow of silence for an indefinite amount of time, only communicating with gestures and writing. There was Mahant Amar Bharti Ji, a famous *urdhvabahu* (arm raised) Baba, who had been holding up one arm for thirty-two years. It is now a shriveled stick of bone with the fingernails growing in all directions (see color plate 8). "It is like a flag raised in honor of Shiva—and once raised, it does not come down."

Then there were the boys, definitely more children than young men, who were nevertheless already full-blown Babas, at least on the surface (see color plate 9). And as Babas they had already developed an appreciation for charas and the wet, deep, nasty-sounding cough that goes along with it. One night a very young boy, a little Baba who had a penchant for posing for photos, sat down by the dhuni and started singing a capella, accompanied only by his little tambourine drum. After the long beautiful, devotional, and slightly melancholic song, he burst into a recital of a series of verses and mantras to the smiling approval of the Babas, who threw money and bits of charas in his lap.

Rampuri told me that what connects most Babas is that they become Babas while they are mere kids. Like Surendra Puri, many of the Babas here knew that they would become Babas at a very young age, and their families, their parents, or their schools couldn't change their minds. In the case of the little singing Baba—his father had come to see Rampuri one day—it was either that or become a petty criminal.

Like all fairs, the Kumbh Mela had an element of entertainment. Several times a day troupes of singers would attend the dhuni and perform, receiving money and charas as payment. For instance, there were the Sakhi, called the *gopis** of Krishna, who were transvestite lovers and devotees of Krishna, men dressed as women in order to be as close as possible to their lord and lover.

One also encountered magic invocations and stage magic, tantra and tan-tricks, and a fair share of fake Babas, con men, and hucksters claiming to have great magical powers, who were less than impressive. There was an aspect of people trying to upstage one another with ever

---

*In Hindu mythology the gopis were milkmaids who fell in love with the young Krishna when he was a *gopala,* or cowherd, in Vrindavan.

more amazing and occasionally macabre "magical" feats. Snake handlers, sword wavers, miracle workers, and everything else you could imagine belonging to the world's biggest magical fair—and more—showed up at the Kumbh Mela. And there were tourist traps aplenty for the spiritual tourist, whether Indian or foreigner. Rampuri's approach to the fake holy men and the people who fell for them was straightforward: "If somebody is smart enough, they will see that somebody is a fake. And if somebody falls for a fake, that means they're not smart enough to see through it, and they deserve what they get. I hate to say it, but this seems to be the reality. Without discrimination, anything goes. And fools deserve what they come up with."

Sometimes the Babas would use their austerity to show off, to demonstrate their control over their bodies and physique in various ways, such as tying their penis several times around a sharp sword, twisting the sword behind their feet, and then having someone *stand* on the sword.

In the context of the Mela, and sitting by the dhuni, there seemed to be nothing especially weird in all of this. Things that would normally cause abhorrence, repulsion, or bewilderment seemed to belong in this strange world. They were part of the furniture.

Fundamentally, what the Babas did was give blessings. People from all castes and walks of life, families, the old and the young, and the rich and the poor, Indians and foreigners alike, all arrived in droves from morning to night to receive blessings from the Babas. Even many of the high-ranking cops and soldiers were devotees. The Babas would give out their blessings by touching people on the forehead and marking their third eye with vibhuti, which they would also give to people to eat. They might also give people some prasad.

There is a common notion in the West that knowledge should be free and equally available to all. In India, this idea does not really exist in practice. There is a tradition of dakshina, of giving wealth or offerings to the guru or tradition as a way of honoring that source of knowledge. This is the way of the esoteric tradition and indeed of Indian culture in general. This tradition is still a confusing issue for many people from outside of India and its traditions and the subject of much debate. In discussing this with Rampuri, I quoted two passages from the Linga Purana about the Kali Yuga: "Masters demean themselves by selling knowledge" and "Sacraments and religion are also for sale."

Rampuri replied: "Knowledge has never been free. When a disciple traditionally goes to a guru, the disciple pays a lot for the knowledge. In fact, he pays everything for the knowledge. He brings dakshina, offerings, wealth to the guru, and even much more than that, he pays for the knowledge with his entire life. So, in fact, traditionally, knowledge is very expensive. The fact that people attempt to sell and buy knowledge with mere money actually demeans the value of the knowledge; that mere money is only a small price that one has to pay for knowledge."

So maybe really an interpretation of that is not that knowledge will be sold, but that knowledge will be sold cheaply. In the tradition, and even in the tantric text, if you read the text in one way or another, by reading the book of the world, by reading the tradition, or by reading the written word, what you will find is that it says, "The pleased guru says to his disciple"—not "the guru," but "the pleased guru." So it's like anything else in the world: if you want something that somebody has, you must please that person. This is the way that it's always worked in the tradition: you must please the guru. You can't be a pain in the ass—the guru doesn't want you around if you're a pain in the ass.

But this is not to say that all the Babas do is act as conduits of knowledge and give out blessings. Just as they are givers of blessings, they are also the throwers of curses. Indeed there was an element of fierceness to the Babas and to the dhuni, a violent intensity that inspired awe and fear in many. In the West, people tend to associate

"Eastern spirituality" (whatever the fuck that means) and yogis with peace and love, with starry-eyed pacifism and feel-good harmony, but looking at these yogis of a genuine ancient tradition you could see how deluded that image actually was in reality. These yogis and Babas were not just ascetics—they were warriors. Traditionally and throughout history Naga Babas have been warriors and even today many of them have a background in the military. There was one Baba, for instance, who enjoyed showing a picture of himself using a metal rod to beat a guy who had falsely claimed to be a Naga Baba.

To call the Naga Babas of the Juna Akhara the "Hell's Angels of Indian spirituality" is really not an overstatement at all. There were definite resemblances—the fraternity, the structure and strict hierarchy, the living by their own laws outside of mainstream society and its norms, the exchange of money, and the violent commitment to the path. As an outsider, or even a welcomed guest and friend, you had better be on your best behavior—you did not want to cross these guys. Mangalanand Puri described the results of such misadventures as follows: "Sometimes when someone does something really bad, they are not just kicked out of the camp or given over to the police, but they are dealt with and punished very severely here inside the Akhara! Here is one example of how serious transgressions are traditionally dealt with here in Juna Akhara: A number of years ago, at a Kumbh Mela, a young sadhu did something seriously forbidden and was caught! He was then severely beaten, his head was half-shaved, he was made a mala of shoes to wear, and all of the black soot of the dirty cooking pots were smeared on his face and body! He was then taken around to all of the dhunis in the Akhara, where his crime was proclaimed, and at each dhuni the Babas beat him with their shoes, and some even beat him with their *chimtas* (tongs used to tend the fire), after which he was thrown out of the Akhara into the street! He was lucky to have escaped with his life!"

"What did he do?" I asked.

"He got drunk and in a fit of anger pissed on his guru."

As in all types of human groups, there were some Babas that were not good guys in the least. Simply wearing ochre, matted locks, and malas and belonging to an order doesn't make one into a nice person. This was even expressed as a literal warning by Rampuri in a serious tone: "There are people here who could eat your liver."

I thought, *Why would they, since they are vegetarians?* but refrained from making such a smart-ass remark. Instead I asked: "Why would anyone want to eat my liver?"

"Because they could. For fun," Rampuri replied.

On certain nights the dhuni also attracted some Aghori Babas. *Ghora* means "darkness," and the *A* negates the word it precedes, so *Aghora* literally means "no darkness." Infamous for their perpetual taboo-breaking and antisocial *sadhana* (spiritual practice), such as nocturnal rituals at cremation grounds involving drinking alcohol from kapala skull bowls, ghosts, possession, sex, drugs, meat eating, sacrifice, and even, some rumor, cannibalism, they are probably among the more extreme of spiritual practitioners in India—like dark mirror images of perpetually smiling, benevolent yogis.

Because their esoteric practices and doctrines lend themselves to easy sensationalism, they have been a source of many articles and documentaries in the West, as well as in India, where during the Mela they were the subject of local newspaper articles as well as reports on the news channels. On the surface, however, it might be hard to tell them apart from the Naga Babas, which is illustrative of how difficult and bewildering it can be to see the differences between the numerous and varied *sampradaya* (initiatory traditions) and sects of India.

In Varanasi, I had visited the central ashram and temple and found it to be little different from other temples. Rampuri explained it thusly: "Huge difference between Aghori and Naga, but not to do with doctrine per se, as one might imagine. Yes, there are doctrinal differences, but that is not what distinguishes the two from each other. It's more an issue of caste. Aghoris are from non-Brahmin and usually lower castes, which means that their universe is not intellectual, as it would be with a Brahmin, the magic is not articulated as a Naga might. These are not things to choose between, as one might choose between a working-class bar and a trendy one. These are sampradayas that one would more naturally belong to because of how—in which caste and condition, and in which geography—one grew up. But one does not really choose because it sounds good."

There was an Aghori practitioner there, however, who was now a Naga Baba. Formerly called Ram Nath, he achieved some kind of infamy after a documentary was made about him and his Aghori practices. From what I gather, Matsyandra Giri, as he is now called, apparently got tired of just hanging out with ghosts at the burning grounds, and so he became part of the Naga Babas.

There was also another Aghori who sometimes sat around the dhuni, drinking chai out of his skull cup. Not a Naga Baba, this particular Aghori had a questionable reputation because of his interest in "helping" Western women with their problems with "boyfriend . . . hasband [sic]." You can imagine that when skull-drinking, ash-garbed yogis tell you that they will help with "troubles with boyfriend," it will usually not involve the boyfriend but may mean something else entirely, something not inspired by wholly altruistic and benevolent thoughts related to their sadhana. This raises the question of just how successful the Babas really are in controlling their sexuality to serve their sadhana and generate tapas. It is hard to say, but the reality remains that when encountering Western women some Babas get their chakras totally tangled up.

One late night at the dhuni, I met a woman, a fellow Finn, who told me her name was Vishvanath. She had a proud, strong, and somewhat crazy spirit that I recognized as distinct to my homeland. To the amusement of the Babas listening, we talked in Finnish, and she told me her story. She lived in Goa with her children most of the year, but they traveled to many important tirthas, including Kedarnath high up in the Himalayas—and now she was with her kids here at the Mela. She showed me a picture of a painting she had photographed at a Nath temple, which, according to her, depicted Väinämöinen, the Finnish shamanic storyteller god. Indeed, the figure looked somewhat like the archetypal image of the Finnish god, with fair skin and gray hair and beard, and even the nature and animals in the picture looked distinctly Nordic.

Vishvanath said that she was a Nath. The Naths, sometimes recognized by their distinctive thick, black earrings, are another distinct sampradaya of Babas, founded by Matsyendranath and given further form by Gorakshanath. The Naths do not recognize caste barriers. Indeed, one of the great Naths was a Westerner, Shri Gurudev Mahendranath (1911–1991), who originally got the advice to delve into the Indian esoteric tradition from Aleister Crowley himself. Rampuri once told me a story of his meeting with Mahendranath, or Dadaji as he was called by the locals. They had sat at his dhuni, and Dadaji had offered to give Rampuri his *maha mantra,* his great mantra, and Rampuri had of course accepted. Dadaji had come closer and solemnly whispered the mantra in Rampuri's ear: "Fuck 'em all."

In addition to all the Babas, devotees, and seekers one encountered at the dhuni, there were, of course, the spectators. They were comprised of mostly Japanese tourists watching from a safe distance, with protective surgical face masks, gloves, and the standard tourist wear of khaki shorts and hiking shoes. Armed with high-quality cameras—and resembling hunters, as Rampuri pointed out—they took shots of the Babas and the dhuni, not desiring anything more than that.

The only way to really learn and understand anything at all of this was to engage and absorb, which in practice meant to sit, watch, and participate, not to make moral, intellectual, or analytical judgments or ask what this or that meant or symbolized, as if all things had implicit and deeper meanings or symbolic values outside of those directly apparent to them—but to simply to sit and watch how things unfolded. And this is what I tried to do. I did not make judgments about anything one way or the other but simply let the experience wash over me to see what knowledge would grow from it.

And so it was that sitting by the dhuni, I became witness to some major events that took place. After lengthy periods of seeming inactivity and sitting around, suddenly there would be a rush of activity, and as if according to some magical logic, big things would happen. There was a gradual opening up of the Akhara taking place, and part of this opening up included the official recognition of the international element within the Akhara and its connection with the rest of the world. This meant that for the first time in the entire history of the ancient order of Naga Babas, three foreigners—Rampuri, Mangalanand Puri, and Vasudev Puri from Italy—were given permanent seating in the ruling council of Juna Akhara and given the title of Shri Mahant, which give them considerably more authority than they had before. And also as a part of this opening up, an Antahrashtriya Mandal, a "World Circle," was established as a means of connecting the Akhara with the world outside of India.

These things were preceded by and took place as a series of events that could be somewhat confusing to an outsider. The governing body of the Juna Akhara met at the dhuni of Shri Maharaj Macchendar Puri to get everyone's signature on the Akhara proclamation made before Guru Dattatreya that these three aforementioned sadhus would now be known as Honored Ones. In a burst of movement, the entourage moved inside the confines of the Maya Devi temple. There, before Guru Dattatreya and Shiva, Juna Akhara secretary Prem Giri Ji made the *pukar,* the proclamation, in which Rampuri, Mangalanand Puri, and Vasudev Puri were each proclaimed Antahrashtriya Mandal ka Shri Mahant. The proclamations were marked and their new status was celebrated by the blowing of the snake-shaped *nagphani* trumpet, as the new Shri Mahants clothed in huge ochre turbans that looked like crowns were adorned with so many flower garlands you could barely see their faces. There was festive mood in the air and everyone present was given garlands of flowers.

Finally the entourage sat down at the Puri dhuni of the courtyard of the Maya Devi temple and had a chillum. Although I could not claim to understand all the things connected to this event, I knew I had witnessed something rare, something that had never happened before in the entire history of the order, and perhaps something that marked the changing times.

Yet, as interesting as these happenings were, everyone was ultimately here for the great bath, the Ganga Snaan. It was the reason for pilgrimage, the moment of culmination, the immersion into the panacea. There were several great baths during the Mela, astrologically significant moments when ordinary water was transformed into amrit, "that which is immortal."

A bathing day was to happen on March 30, but nobody—not even the Naga Babas themselves—knew if there was going to be a procession of the Naga Babas. The day before, I had tried to find out something about what would possibly take place, but everyone seemed to have their own ideas. I heard that some Babas not of the Juna Akhara were going to make a procession, such as the Vaishnavas (the followers of Vishnu), many of whom had padlocked their penises away as an austerity—the "locks on cocks" as I called them.

Nevertheless, on the morning of the day of the bath I was sitting at the dhuni when three Brahmin pandits arrived from Ujjain, Varanasi, and someplace else. A small troupe consisting of Rampuri, Mangalanand Puri, Savitri Puri, Yogananda Puri, Surendra Puri, and a few other Babas and devotees quickly gathered and followed the priests through the labyrinthine Akhara toward the river Ganga.

We arrived at the secluded Bhairava Ghat (Bhairava is a fierce manifestation of Shiva), where only Babas are allowed to bathe, and here we would take our snaan (see color plate 10). I took my dip thrice in the waters of the Ganga, under the watchful eye and guidance of the Babas.

As I went under the water, I could feel the strong current of the Ganga and the current of this age-old tradition sweep through me. Emerging from under the water, I lifted my cupped hands in a salute to the river and the sun, the drops of the water glistening in the radiance of the light.

Then under the guidance of the three Brahmin priests, and with our feet still immersed in the water of the Ganga, we took part in a puja in which an icon of Dattatreya was bathed in the river and then decorated and showered with offerings of water, flowers, rice, sweets, colored paste, malas, and garlands. Afterward we sat on the stairs of the Bhairava Ghat, taking refuge from the scorching sun. A Naga Baba came up to me, pointed to the ring on his cock put there as an austerity, and smiled proudly.

People from outside of the tradition reacted to these events at the Akhara and to the Kumbh Mela in general in very different ways, depending on their perspective, background, intent, and cultural discourse. Some people were put off by the strong emphasis placed on dakshina at the Akhara, and the all the talk, exchange, and counting of money that occurred. Some thought it resembled a spiritual mafia, which, in a way, it did. Others were put off by the sheer intensity of the Mela, the kooky Babas, the endless crowds, the chaos and noise, the magnitude of it all. One man said to me: "This is not for us. We are Scandinavians; we are forest people."

Some people felt exactly the opposite. Having heard the call of the yogic path so strongly and for a long while, for them all this was like coming home. They had given themselves over to the extraordinary world of the Naga Sannyasis with such abandonment that all doubt went out the window. These people were my friends Yogananda Puri and Savitri Puri, who had organized the retreat in Sweden that I had participated in earlier. Both had been practicing and teaching hatha yoga and had been part of the Western yoga movement for more than ten years. Even though their approach to yoga was more esoteric than Pattabhi Jois's ashtanga yoga, which emphasizes physical fitness, they had also seen and experienced the limitations of how yoga was presented and understood in the West. To them, the Naga tradition, "however chaotic, insane and seemingly mad it appeared, offered some understanding and sanity in this crazy world and time that we are living in." Both were to undertake the traditional panch guru initiation into Naga Sannyasis, "the sacrament of the five gurus," and the Virja Havan, the Heroic Sacrifice.

I saw Savitri Puri the day following her initiation. She had lost her voice in all the excitement, her head was shaved, and her forehead was marked with yellow and red paste. Her face and being gleamed with the aura of a newborn, overwhelmed with joy, bliss, fear, and respect. Yogananda Puri was to have his great rite in a few days—the cutting away, the last rites.

Going through initiation into *sannyas,* an ordinary person becomes transformed into a mythic being of the extraordinary world, where different laws are in effect than those of the ordinary world. The chela joins the company of gods and demons, spirits and ghosts. He is no longer a part of his biological family but gains a new family and lineage via the esoteric tradition of which he becomes a part, whose progenitor is Dattatreya himself. It is at the Kumbh Mela that the procreation and strengthening of these families occurs. In a great chain of succession starting from the progenitor of the lineage himself, the chela aims to *become* the guru, adopting his knowledge and his personality and sometimes even being possessed by his spirit. It follows that the concept of individuality, which holds such preoccupation in the West, does not really hold the same position in this tradition, where one aims to embody the tradition. To illustrate this, one day at the dhuni Rampuri (himself possessed by his guru Hari Puri Baba) pointed out to me yet another Baba who also claimed possession by the spirit of a long-dead guru.

Indeed, it was getting a little intense for me too at times. I took off to Rishikesh, a few hours' ride away, to rest and recharge for a couple

Fig. 4.1. The author at Rampuri's dhuni with
Mangalanand Puri and Rampuri
(Photograph by Christian Möllenhoff)

of days. It was a relaxing contrast to the often chaotic hustle and bustle of Hardwar and the Mela. I was also glad to meet my friends Vijaya Puri and Lars there, from Germany and Denmark respectively, who had been ill in Hardwar and needed a respite from all of it. On my first night, I sat on the balcony of the Swiss cottage-style guesthouse and marveled at the majestic mountains that rose high enough to almost cover the moon. There was a warm breeze in the night air, birds sang, and occasionally dogs barked. It was serene in comparison to Hardwar. The Ganga flowed through the valley below, as it seems to flow through all things in India.

Wandering down into the valley, I could see another chasm of difference between this world and that of Hardwar. Whereas Hardwar was an ancient place of power and represented a traditional Indian esoteric tradition, Rishikesh was like a spiritual pick-and-choose marketplace, a New Age haven with all the crystals, yoga classes, strange "Swedish" massages, esoteric bookshops, tarot card readers, and organic, vegan food shops you'd ever need—if you happened to be into that sort of thing. A shoddily handwritten sign said: "Visit for Meditation, Philosophy, Answers to Spiritual Questions, Indology, Galactic Chronicles."

Rishikesh was also crowded with a particular brand of foreign travelers—the smug neohippies that sport a strange kind of hip arrogance and a steady stoned gaze, and who often wander around scantily clothed and behaving in an inappropriate manner, giving Westerners the reputation they sometimes have and affecting how foreigners are treated (for example, being denied entry to many temples). Perhaps it was the unfortunate bastard legacy of The Beatles, and the clichéd "quest to find oneself in the East" that had resulted in this. It was to Rishikesh that The Beatles famously came looking for that great something. At the behest of George Harrison they arrived here to study transcendental meditation at the ashram of Maharishi Mahesh Yogi, located just across from where I was staying. The ashram now lies abandoned and swallowed by the forest. Although The Beatles composed much of their brilliant *White Album* here, they did not, it seems, find what they were looking for—except maybe for Harrison, whose ashes were scattered into the river Ganga when he died. And that, too, epitomizes something of the Westerners' quest in the East: often they return to their country even more lost than they were when they first set out on their journey.

Nevertheless, we walked down to the sandy banks of Ganga for the evening aarti ceremony. A traditional Indian band played devotional music. From a young boy we bought incense and some floating ghee lamps made out of leaves and decorated with flowers. I pushed the burning light into the river and watched it quietly float away among the many others, forming a solemn parade of little lights against the darkness of the night.

The next night, the Dalai Lama was to appear in an evening puja by the Ganga in Rishikesh, meaning that all traffic was blocked and there was a general buzz going on. But being tired of all the endless ceremonies and especially the endless crowds, I chose not to go. Instead I bought some beer outside of the city limits and stayed on the balcony of my guesthouse, drinking and watching the sun set beyond the mountains. The Dalai Lama seemed too far removed from my life to even approach except as a mere curiosity. Besides, the Dalai Lama was never one of my heroes. A doctrine or an idea without force to back it up remains an abstraction; *passive resistance* simply means to let one be trampled over. Sitting on the terrace overlooking the vast, dark ranges, I wondered where my journeys had taken me.

Soon I was back in Hardwar. It was early morning and I was at the dhuni when my mother called. Somehow I knew instantly, before answering, what it was. After a long illness and a recent fall, my father had died.

I sat down by the roots of a tall tree opposite the dhuni and listened to my mother's words. Birds were singing in the morning and the sky was a bright blue. The silent Baba walked by and stopped to gesture something to me with a wide smile.

In a detached, surreal state I walked back along the Niranjani Akhara road to the resort by the Ganga where I stayed. I opened a bottle of whiskey and poured the first libation for my father. Then I sat down by the Ganga and drank. Death washed over me as thick and wide as the ancient current of the river by which I was sitting, and I wept.

Around noon I was joined by my friend Christian. He was a Swedish yoga teacher, the same age as me, and we had received the same initiation. He had also lost his mother in a car accident only a few weeks earlier. So there we sat by the shore of the Ganga, listening to bittersweet songs, watching the river flow by, and drinking whiskey, two men equally overwhelmed by the loss of our progenitors, by the sorrow, the beauty, the magic, by the profundity of life and death. How raw is the fabric of reality when touched by tragedy. Sorrow is a reality, a sobering realization, bound to touch us during our life, no matter how we may wish to hide behind a facade built to protect us from such unpleasant things.

Rampuri, having heard the news, told me before I could say anything: "Now you take the first flight home. This is what you do." I bought the first ticket I could get. I knew that this was to be the Kumbh Mela for me.

In the evening I wandered down the streets in solitude before visiting the dhuni. How things took on a different, surreal perspective in light of death. I sat down and watched the blinking lights and the people rushing by. On the Niranjani Akhara road I bought the best and sweetest things I could find to give to the Babas by the dhuni: something *gur* (sweet) for the gurus. Arriving at the dhuni, I gave my offerings and sat down in silence. A few friends and Babas gave me a knowing look.

A week earlier I had talked with an Indian man who had just conducted his mother's cremation, dressed all in white with his head shaved. As we smoked cigarettes on a balcony overlooking the Ganga, he said he was here to conclude the funeral rites. Indeed death was something very characteristic of the Kumbh Mela. Babas, yogis, devotees, and ordinary people came here to die. In an act of final defiance and a show of divine power, great Babas could sometimes choose their own time of death, announce it beforehand, and then "leave their body" at will. Their bodies would then be carried around, still sitting cross-legged, decorated with garlands of marigolds, with malas in their hands and with money thrown on their lap. It was, according to the tradition, an auspicious time to die. Perhaps because of this, death was not a stranger, nor was it treated as such—neither with overly visible grief or sentimentality.

Disconnected from the normal talk at the dhuni, I wandered wearily through the alleys of the Akhara. An ash-covered Naga Baba waved me over, and I stumbled toward him. I paid my respects to his dhuni and to him and sat down. Skyclad in his ashen attire he offered me food and smiled deeply. Not conversant enough in Hindi to engage in dialogue, I simply sat there with him, the ash-covered smiling Baba.

Before dawn the next day, just as the sun was slowly beginning to rise, I had my final bath in the Ganga in deep silence, as did my friend Christian. I felt the cold water over my head and body, and the pull of the river. With my feet in the water, I raised my hands skyward, toward the rising sun, and felt the stream of life and death rinse over me, as endless flowers and garlands flowed past. I was at the edge of worlds that was this river—an edge between the ordinary and the extraordinary, between end and beginning. On another level, I was beholding the transformative edge that this time and place represented, and its eventual crossing over. And yet, this here was not an edge for me to cross. I felt the call of my own lineage and lands, the rivers and the sea, the call of my own blood and the gods that dwelt therein. I washed my feet, hands, and head with Ganga water, filled some containers with it, and said my good-byes.

As we walked toward the Juna Akhara for the last time, I distributed coins and notes of money to the rows of beggars and sadhus that gather along the road in the early morning. To one of the young Naga Babas at Rampuri's dhuni, I gave my pocket watch that the little guy had been admiring; he in turn gave me one of his malas, a red rosary made of plastic. This was my day of departure and the last time I was to visit the dhuni. It was also the very day Yogananda was to have his grand initiation into a Naga Sannyasi, a Naga Baba. He was to have his last rites, as I was to have mine.

Again I brought some sweets and my last dakshina to the dhuni and received the blessings and a mark on my third eye with vibhuti, orange and red paste. It was the day of funeral rites, and Rampuri was talking to Yogananda Puri: "We are cutting away ties. Cutting ties with family, with caste, with the past life, with the ordinary world. Cutting away," Rampuri said, making a scissorlike gesture with his fingers.

Rampuri told me to come and sit close to him and the dhuni. Both he and Mangalanand Puri told me: "Take some water from the Ganga and bring it home to sprinkle on your father and say a prayer for his spirit to reach the highest heavens. This is why you have come here: traveling all the way to India to discover that you have to return to your homeland and put your father to rest. This is your Kumbh Mela. This is the puja you must perform. The last rites." And so this I did.

A month later, back in Helsinki, there was a heavy downpour of rain when my father's coffin was finally lowered into the earth. I poured a bottle of amrit, the nectar of immortality, on his casket. The celestial waters mixed with the rain and tears, and all that water in turn mixed with the soil on and around my father, as sky met earth.

I once had a dream-vision of death. I was in a large old house on the shore of a vast ocean that was made out of a claylike material, earthen red in color. The air and ground was warm as I walked barefoot up the stairs to the highest floor, dressed in white. Arriving at the top, I saw from the large openings in the walls that it was either dawn or dusk—the kind of liminal state where everything is colored to a golden red by the sun, and yet the sun itself is not visible. There was no fear, no confusion, no sadness, nothing longed for—only a feeling of returning to some primal home. I stepped out of the opening in the wall and simply drifted along a warm ocean breeze toward the ocean and the purple clouds above it, eventually vanishing there completely, into the mist above the sea. This is how I choose to see my father's death.

A few weeks after returning home I was fortunate enough to meet Savitri Puri, who was still in a state of post-initiatory afterglow. Because of the eruption of a volcano in Iceland that had effectively shut down all air traffic in Europe for weeks, Savitri was on her way overland to Denmark, having arrived in Helsinki via a train from Moscow. She told me about the last, concluding days of the Mela and what had happened on the final major bathing day on April 14. By that day, vastly surpassing all expectations, approximately 40 million people had arrived at the Hardwar Kumbh Mela area between Jwalapur and Rishikesh. And on that day, 16 million pilgrims took a holy bath in the Ganga. Apparently, a well-known Baba (not from the Juna Akhara) had been late with his procession and in his haste had resorted to a shortcut or taken a wrong turn. As a result his entourage had collided with another procession in progress. Because of this, a barrier had broken and seven people, including a child, had fallen and had been trampled to death. They called it a "karmic tragedy." After hearing of this, the head of the Juna Akhara had announced that the Naga Babas of the Juna Akhara would not take part in the marching and the grand procession, being the only Akhara not to participate. Shortly afterward, the great fair was declared over.

Looking back at the Kumbh Mela, I am aware that I experienced something that perhaps is disappearing in its current form, belonging to an age of the past. How the future Kumbh Melas will take shape is difficult to tell, but I doubt it will be similar to what I experienced much longer. Perhaps then, such Melas will be the source of tale and legend.

How the Kumbh Mela affected the various participants, how the experience was churned into knowledge, and how the magic manifested itself is yet another chapter in the ever-unfolding story. In the end, a magic mirror was found and gazed into, revealing knowledge of the inner and outer worlds, of "self" and "other." And in the end, perhaps even in a more profound sense, the magic mirror broke. While breaking, it revealed a deeper truth: the merging of "self" and "other," which are not opposites but a unity reflective of each other. And in gazing into that shattered mirror, the realization that in me were deeper vistas than could be ever found in this foreign land.

To truly know something, one needs to be within touching distance of the thing one desires to know. Insight and knowledge do not require beliefs or ideologies, as those things can indeed just make them even more shrouded. Insight and knowledge can be gleaned from written words, but profound knowledge requires participation in firsthand experience. It requires one to have sense experience of the object of knowledge, beyond the realm of the mere intellect.

The knowledge I acquired from delving into the traditional Indian esoteric tradition, I learned via personal experience. It has required participation and usage for it to become active. It is also nothing I could fully explain in written words, even if I tried. And such knowledge requires pilgrimage. To have knowledge of the source, one has to travel to the source, or be satisfied by the streams that flow from that source, eventually becoming more polluted, more impure, as they get farther away from it. To truly know the story, one has to become the story.

**Plate 1.** "Burning is learning—all is ash." The author in Varanasi, India.
(Photograph by A. Haapapuro)

**Plate 2.** Framed pictures sold to pilgrims, depicting the central murtis
(sculptures of deities) at Dakshinkali (Photographs by unknown photographer)

**Plate 3.** Aarti puja at Pashupathinath: in the foreground a young Brahmin pandit conducts the puja, while the Naga Baba remains seated (Photograph by A. Haapapuro)

**Plate 4.** The giant, wrathful Kal Bhairav, one of Shiva's numerous forms, at Hanuman Dhoka, Durbar Square, Kathmandu; pilgrims can be seen laying offerings at his feet (Photograph by A.Haapapuro)

**Plate 5.** Row of Shiva lingams in Pashupatinath, Kathmandu
(Photograph by A. Haapapuro)

**Plate 6.** Altar at Dattatreya shrine, featuring several murtis of the gods, Shiva lingams, and offerings. In the center is Guru Dattatreya, whose three heads are those of Brahma, Vishnu, and Shiva. (Photograph by the author)

**Plate 7.** The dhuni during the Kumbh Mela in Hardwar. Surrounding the dhuni are pictures from the Puri family of Babas. Surrounding the fire are a trishul of Shiva decorated with marigolds, a damaru drum, kamandal water pots, and the chimtas-tongs that are used to tend the fire. Under a picture of Dattaryea sits Rampuri, who presides over the dhuni. The smiling Baba on the left is Mangalanand Puri. The author is on the bottom left, and next to him is Savitri Puri. (Photograph by Christian Möllenhoff)

**Plate 8.** Amar Bharti Ji Maharaj, an urdhvabahu ("raised arm")
Baba by the dhuni. He has kept his arm raised for
Shiva for more than thirty years. (Photograph by the author)

**Plate 9.** Young Naga Baba of the Juna Akhara in Hardwar (Photograph by the author)

**Plate 10.** Babas relaxing at the Bhairava Ghat after bathing in the Ganga. Surendra Puri is seated on the left. (Photograph by the author)

**Plate 11.** Kalaripayat practitioners in Fort Kochi, Kerala. The man applying the joint lock suffered from polio as a child. (Photograph by Justine Cederberg)

**Plate 12.** Standing stones at Lejre, Roskilde, Denmark (Photograph by Justine Cederberg)

**Plate 13.** Thor on top of the old Carlsberg brewery, Copehagen, Denmark
(Photograph by Justine Cederberg)

# 5
# THE RIVER OF STORY

*I have told you all that constitutes the very core of Truth;*
*There is no you, no me, no superior being, no disciple, no*
*    Guru.*
*The nature of supreme Reality is self-evident and simple;*
*I am nectarean knowledge, unchanging bliss;*
*I am everywhere, like space.*

AVADHUT GITA, CHAPTER 3, VERSE 42

I SIT AT A CORNER CAFÉ off Boulevard Saint-Michel by the river Seine, watching the steady hum in the streets of Paris, the pulse in the arteries of this old, jaded city. There is a certain light that attracts me here—the way the sun settles over the houses and rooftops, the way the churches and temples glow ochre in stark contrast to the deep blue night sky. In this mythical city of light by an equally mythical river flowing through it all, something feels familiar or reoccurring. It seems I am always walking in the shadows of old gods still lingering at the limits of a modern world. Sometimes stumblingly, I pierce the veil to the catch a glimpse of the sacred, which lies just below the surface of everything, and yet remains ever elusive. And Pan smiles, unmoved, playing his flutes at the Jardin du Luxembourg.

In my broken French, I order Cognac and cast a glance into the river of past, present, and future. *Vu de l'extérieur*—a view from the outside, as I have into many things. It has been more than two years since I was in India at the Kumbh Mela. Equally, time has passed since I have seen my friends from that world—the Babas, yogis, chelas, and *sadhakas.* Earlier today, after having spent a magical morning and afternoon in Disneyland with my niece, I went to meet my friends Surendra Puri and Christian at a yoga center in Paris. I arrived late in the evening and the puja had been concluded. Surendra Puri was holding court on his central mat, opposite the altar and surrounded by those in attendance. As I went to greet him in the traditional manner by touching his feet (or the place where his feet connected with the earth), he in turn instantly grabbed me in his arms and embraced me. Then he smiled in his familiar deep, disarming style and said, "Good to see you, dear Adinath Puri Ji!" He put a bindu on my third eye with yellow and orange paste and sprinkled some rice on my forehead. "We are family," he said, while tying a red cord around my right wrist, and calling out for prasad to offer us.

How different people's journeys in life can be to possibly the same, elusive end. Surendra Puri is about my age but has led a vastly different existence. Early in his youth he had taken the path of the ultimate renunciate, living alone in a forest with no home and no possessions and feeding off of whatever was growing in nature. He did this for several *years,* which might seem unfathomable to us, the civilized, urban consumers. He had practiced his sadhana with a fierce severity that would make many would-be master Western magicians run for their protective circles. And yet his presence was anything but severe; it was rather warm, playful, and empathic.

In a gentle and hushed tone, he told a story about when, a long time ago, under the guidance of his guru, he had meditated over a corpse in a burial ground for several nights in a row: "I was very scared, naked. Much bones. Repeating mantras. I was really happy the corpse did not suddenly rise up. But I knew my guru was there, so nothing very bad would happen."

Again, this brings up a central problem we face in the West. For the most part, we lack our own gurus—that is, teachers and guides with a voice of authority and the power reflecting an ancient, unbroken tradition. Our traditions have been severed, and the access we too seldom gain to them is through highly suspicious entities, whether modern ones or those claiming ancient lineages.

We are also told that our own spiritual and magical traditions are irrelevant and outdated. Instead we are offered a range of religions, ideologies, and creeds from which we can pick and choose whatever might interest us on an ideal, aesthetic, but ultimately superficial level. As we lack context and handles, we stumble along in a jungle of abstract ideas written in dark chambers by pale intellectuals and lifeless scholars, surrounding ourselves with dry academia, baseless New Age books, and countless feel-good courses and self-help guides, mostly of thoroughly modern origin. We seek authenticity, fiddle around with this or that esoteric discipline, dabble in dark shit, and sometimes plunge headlong into the abyss with perhaps no one there to catch us. When we resurface from the other worlds, sometimes instead of gifts we bring back with us psychic scars and holes in our souls—not to mention massively inflated egos.

Let it be restated: yogis and Babas are living links in an ancient line of knowledge, of wisdom not confined to a book or creed, but spoken and sung through countless mouths since time immemorial. Yogis are the guardians of this line, which in India is called Sanatan Dharma, the eternal tradition and the laws of nature and the cosmos. What yogis do is act as conduits of magic, the blessings of nature, rooted in this ancient tradition of knowledge, for the people that seek and come to them. *Ideally,* at least, they bring happiness, prosperity, and wisdom into people's lives. They are also the great storytellers, reflecting the story told again and again in myth and legend and long before they were written down. They tell of the quest of the hero—that is, the journey of the true human being.

Ever since I can remember, great stories have been a central part of my life. They have provided a narration and a map to this long, strange voyage. My earliest memories revolve around my grandmother telling me fairy tales, legends, and stories. Although the details of these have been dimmed in my memory by time, I can still remember many of their motifs. And I can remember my grandmother, rocking back and forth calmly in her rocking chair, smoking while telling me tales and reading to me, bathing me in the river of story. In my mind's eye I see a great red book, massive in my little hands, with time-worn pages and black-and-white pictures of dark woods, castles, monsters, beautiful maidens, and many other strange and wonderful things. And stories upon stories of heroes and villains, of great epic journeys, of quests and hidden treasures.

The imprint these stories left on my spirit is undeniable. They stirred my soul. I would play in the nearby woods with a bow and arrows and a small sword. The stories of my grandmother would be inevitably linked with my adventures and games. I would search for treasures and bury some of my own for others to find. And in my games, I always played the part of the hero, of course. I would like to think that much has not changed from that.

These little stories were and are connected to the Great Story, which is not new, but the oldest story there is. This story is written on the surface of the Earth and reflected in the hemisphere of the starry sky. In this day and age, we still have stories and we still have games, but the storytellers themselves—the bards, the shamans, the wise elders, the keepers of memory and lore, the links in the great chain—are fast disappearing, rowing their boats out to the ocean. And we are left on the shore, staring into the mist at the edge of worlds.

All this goes well beyond yoga, Sanatan Dharma, or India.

When we were talking about this subject with Rampuri some years back, he said: "Speaking of your country . . . I saw this painting the last time I was there that really opened my eyes to Finland. What I saw, if I might just spend a second describing it: we see a forest that has been chopped down and cleared of all trees, except for one. And this one tree has been cut and is lying on the ground. There is a musical instrument that is resting upon this tree that is cut down—obviously no one is playing it. Nobody is in the foreground of the picture.

And next to this instrument and the tree is a small fire that looks like it is smoldering and going out. Off in the distance, we see a number of people that have gathered on a hill and they seem to be building something. Now, when I saw that, I knew immediately what they were building: it was a church. And I could see that the spirits of the forest had left, that the storyteller had left his instrument behind him and was gone, that the fire was very quickly going out, and yet people were gathering at a distance on a hill to build something of man. This was very revealing to me of the culture of Finland and the time (I believe he painted this at the end of the nineteenth century). And so I could see that here was a calling to somehow return, not to go backward in time when I say *return,* but rather an embracing of that substance and that foundation that lies beneath the surface in the culture, in the land, of Finland. If I could be somehow useful in giving people a means of reembracing that spirit of the land, then I would consider my work to be very successful."

Rampuri is of course describing a classic work by Akseli Gallén-Kallela, *Heathendom and Christendom* (original title: *Pakanuus ja kristinusko*). The storyteller that has departed is Väinämöinen, one of the central archetypal shamanic figures and gods in the Finnish mythos. It is Väinämöinen who with his instrument, the kantele, sings the world into being with his runes, while gods and spirits from all worlds gather around to listen. The forest, once the temple of the holy that came into

Fig. 5.1. *Heathendom and Christendom* by Akseli Gallén-Kallela,
sketch for the cupola frescoes of the Finnish Pavilion in Paris, 1899,
gouache on paper, 146 x 152 cm, Antell collections,
Finnish National Gallery/Ateneum Art Museum
(Photograph by Hannu Aaltonen)

being from Väinämöinen's song, is cut down, being reduced to a mere gross resource.

This is historical fact: one of the prime agendas of the Christian religion newly arrived to Finland was to cut down the holy trees and sacred groves to sever the relationships and cut the connections that the folk had to the land. The mythic songs of the gods played on the kantele have been mostly abandoned and forgotten. The fire of story-telling, that is, the wisdom that lies in ancestral memory and knowledge, a way of seeing and *reading* the world passed down since ancient times, is fast going out, and mere embers remain. We are left standing alone in an arid desert with the arbitrary and abstract constructions of man.

The painting by Gallén-Kallela speaks to us clearly about this vacuity and disconnection that lies at the root of the many ills of our age. Something essential has been lost in our role and interaction with the natural world, and perhaps most of all in ourselves. However, the magical instrument has been left behind for future generations, so they may once more play the divine songs in times of dire need, and the departed king may return.

Beyond a doubt, we need our gods and our sense of them to rejoin us. How this might be done is still a matter of great concern and debate. There is no going back to past forms, nor is there any sense in being nostalgic about the outer trappings of yesterday. To somehow rekindle the essence may be all that matters; we can only move ever forward. We have to become the hero of our own story, both in our personal lives and as a collective. All this might sound like a cliché, but in today's post-whatever culture, it seems most truths are. We have to dig deep into our roots, into the recesses of our soul and simultaneously have our vision into the future. The slumbering embers of the dying fire need to be brought back to a smoldering flame in order to guide us through a very dark age indeed, the Kali Yuga revealing itself all around us.

The mythical and magical place into which I entered in India is closing. I wrote in the last chapter of my story that the world that I encountered in the Kumbh Mela was one that was disappearing in its current form, as it seemed to belong to a past age. I realized that I had my foot in the door to a place whose entrances are being shut and are ever harder to find.

This closing world is being sealed off from the inside and the outside. Already parts of the melas are moving indoors, camps and tents abandoned, and modern technology at the fair is increasing. The Kumbh is being partially broadcast live on TV and the Internet, and indeed TVs can be seen present at some of the Babas' dhunis. Stories told by the fire are being replaced by dramatic renditions watched on TV; the direct, visceral experience is replaced by the vicarious. How long and how much the melas will remain untouched by the gnawing teeth of the changing times and the onslaught of modernization remains to be seen.

To the obvious dismay of the Juna Akhara, some Naga Babas of the order have left their vocation as sadhus to become householders or to get married, sometimes in the West. I do not claim to have the answers to the questions this has raised recently, but one thing is clear: as with so many areas related to India and its traditions, and the complex, multifaceted issues surrounding it, dichotomical, dualistic thinking and valuing will get us nowhere. This line of thinking, which simplistically pits one side against another in moralistic fashion, "good versus evil," is glaringly and equally prevalent among Western yogic practitioners and some Babas.

It seems the words in the last chapter of my story have rung especially true in light of recent events. Perhaps partially as a backlash to the times and circumstances within the order, the Juna Akhara has effectively banned entry of foreigners into their camp at the next Kumbh Mela. To protect its sacred and ancient tradition from modernity, progress, and globalism, it has closed its gates to the influence of outsiders and mlecchas. This probably does not affect foreigners already initiated into to the order or connected to it, but it certainly will make things harder for those seeking entry from the outside. But perhaps this is as it should be. Perhaps this is to be taken as a statement that people should seek out their own sacred traditions, seek out the divine on the land they are standing on, and connect with the streams of knowledge dormant in their own blood.

The Kumbh Mela I took part in had affected my *guru bhais** in various ways. It seemed that for most, magic had happened. Christian, with whom I had shared whiskey and tears at the Ganga while we mourned over our newly departed parents, had moved to Paris, founded a yoga center (L'école Yoga et Méditation Paris), and gotten married. Vijaya Puri, who had heartbreakingly told me about the almost nonexistent chances for her and her husband to ever conceive a child, had become pregnant shortly after the Kumbh and had given birth to a magical son suitably named Merlin. Yogananda Puri and Savitri Puri had made the heroic sacrifice and become chelas, joining the ranks of the extremely rare Naga Babas of Western origin.

For Savitri Puri at least, this transition from her former self to a Naga Baba had been far from easy and painless. For her, the crossing of the threshold was comparable to a snake shedding its skin. She wrote to me that upon returning from India she had been lost, confused, and overwhelmed, "almost wanting to leave her body." Slowly, however, she had started growing into her new personality, writing that even if it was and still is difficult, it has also been a great opportunity for learning and knowledge and for deconstructing her old personality. She continued as follows: "The way this happens is from engagement, not withdrawal. This took me some time to be able to commit to. And it is not engagement with anything or anyone, it is an engagement with the new family of which my new person belongs to, and with my Guru, who not

---

*Guru bhai* means "spiritual brothers" and students of the same guru.

only is the authority for me, but a Western man who has already gone through these things himself."

It seemed that for Savitri Puri, as for most of us, the struggle is between engagement and withdrawal. And ultimately, between love and fear. As for myself, I certainly had my share of the struggle. In the aftermath of the death of my father and the natural end of my more formal relationship with Rampuri, I began a phase of my life that was marked by an inward turning. In a sense, I had lost two fathers at the same time—the biological and the spiritual. The magic show was over, the curtains drawn, and the lights switched on. A great wave of novelty had gushed over everything, and now it was receding back into itself. "You have been disconnected," said the voice on the other end. My life became weary. Disillusionment, despair, and depression grew to be my intimate companions and the *vrittis,* the endless, circular fluctuations of the mind, were not foreigners to my being. I had reached the end of many paths then and wondered where all my pilgrimages had really taken me. And what, if anything, I had to show for them.

There are stories within stories that are sometimes left untold, words whispered only in the dark of night. One such tale involves the first chapter of my story. By chance or by destiny, I connected with a woman during my first journey in India. On the last morning before returning home, looking over the unusually tranquil sea, she cried silently. I did not then understand why. Some time later she was diagnosed with cancer and lay dying in the hospital. Looking back on it now, I felt as if she had some awful premonition of the future. When I next saw her, she was weak and her head was shaved. We gazed out of the window, high above the dreary, winter-gray city into the nothingness. "Are you happy," she asked me. "No," I said. You do not lie to a dying person. We walked down the quiet corridor of the cancer ward. That was the last time I saw her alive.

I have been to hell. It is an endless, white hospital hall, lined with the suffering and the dying, being told that this is it. Whether the dark corridors at a refuge for lepers in Kathmandu or the sterile white walls of Helsinki, I sometimes see these vistas of deep sadness and bone-crushing suffering stretching into infinity. This is a vision I still struggle with greatly. But perhaps this is the eternal struggle we all face as human beings. And sometimes, even when the odds are against us, we have to fight.

A yoga teacher in Delhi once said to me that my "aura is surrounded by darkness." How right she may have been. But it is not through shunning darkness that we come to know light, but only through delving into it. I have always sought to be winged both in the sun and the moon. But in the process, I have certainly taken a plunge headlong into the depths. My consciousness has been plagued by many illusions, locked in limitations, and paralyzed by fear. Kali is shown holding her hand in the *mudra* marking "no fear"—and yet I have been afraid. I have had recurring dreams, visions, and thoughts of being alone in a mechanistic universe, just another piece of meat on the line waiting for the inevitable knife. I have felt separated from others and cut off from union with the divine.

All of these things have come and gone. I have watched them approach and witnessed them leave. Sometimes I have even been attached to them. I have learned that much can be gained by simply letting go of things. Emotions and memories, spiritual or magical paths, identities or aspects of one's personality, material items and objects—it is all just stuff in the end. Following the classic model of many traditions, one starts from simplicity based on a lack of knowledge. Gradually one gains experience and knowledge, and slowly, one moves toward ever more complexity. But in the end, one has to let go of all that one has learned and return to simplicity. This is what I have done. The process I have undergone since the Kumbh has been one of deconstruction and simplification. Instead of an accumulation of more knowledge, it has been a letting go, a reduction of excess baggage. I have set my sight on the core and seed of things. From the depths, I have turned my gaze upward, reaching for the brilliant radiance at the surface.

Many years ago in Varanasi I was given a prophecy of my life. I was sitting with a friend by the Manikarnika Ghat, watching the endless burning corpses, when an Indian man engaged us in conversation. He told us there was a great Baba living in a shack nearby, who was proficient in astrology and could tell us many things. Of course, we did not believe him at all. But Varanasi being the city of thieves, we thought it would be an experience at least, and so we found ourselves sitting on the shitty floor of his shack with the eager Indian already rubbing his palms in anticipation. The old white-clad, gray-haired and bearded Baba eventually arrived, and after what seemed like endless hassling about money, the session started. The Baba told me many things about myself and my life to come, as he saw it written on my hands, my face, and the stars. He related to me my characteristics as they pertained to my life, love, passions, creative work, dispositions, and such. He foretold the progression and unfolding of events. Although he was right about several things, at the time we laughed it all off.

Some eight years later, I recalled some of the things that the Baba had foretold, and I found and listened to the tape on which I had recorded parts of his words. I was surprised to discover that more of it was true than I would have thought. This is telling of how India was and still is for me partially an enigma, a sign that there is some magic in this world.

And so it often goes in life. Just when I think that the game is up, there comes a magic touch. The nature of the universe has revealed itself to me in an experience, telling me that we are not separate after all. Suddenly, all paths are again open for me. The magic is there, as it always was, as long as I invoke it. And then I hear the song of Dattatreya, the bringer of the teachings and giver of initiation:

*Truly, it is by the grace of God*
*That the knowledge of Unity arises within.*
*Then a man is released at last*
*from the great fear of life and death.*

AVADHUT GITA, CHAPTER 1, VERSE 1

Back in Paris, we sat around the altar with Surendra Puri for sat-sang. We talked about many things, and one area was the ever-alluring Tantra. Tantra, the union of Shiva and Shakti, is viewed with much suspicion and fear in modern India. Equally dubious in the West, it has manifested as a series of silly New Age "sensual and spiritual" erotic exercises. Someone exemplified this recently by asking me about my story: "Is there tantric sex stuff in there?"

In response to the recent upheavals in the Juna Akhara involving some Naga Babas leaving the sadhu life to become householders and marry, Surendra Puri had a curious comment: "The love is the same, but the thought is different." His words rang in my head long after that, and I pondered what he meant.

There might not be a word more frivolously used than *love*. The word *love* has become banal and devalued, a marketplace manipula-tive commodity used as an easy emotional trigger. An entire culture exists around this mushy, adolescent, and juvenile kind of love. Rather than something ever expansive and connecting, this love is often rooted in fear, in a strange kind of desperation. And yet, despite all of these things, love is still one of the quintessential human qualities that marks us as beings reaching for something beyond ourselves.

I reread my story about India and thought about how much love played a part in it. I, too, have experienced love gained and love lost. I, too, have witnessed the joy of love coming into being and the agony of love dying. But is there another kind of love, a deeper kind of love, a love that remains?

Union is the essence of life and is the creative force of the universe.

Fig. 5.2. The author and Surendra Puri in Paris
(Photograph by Christian Möllenhoff)

This union is manifested in human terms as love. Possibly the highest kind of love is that between two souls that see each other as reflections of one another, as part of the same spirit. In this light, one's object of love becomes one's teacher, the highest embodiment of the divine. Worship takes form as *seva* (service). In the case of lovers, sex becomes a sacrament in emulation of Shiva and Shakti. But it is not an easy path. One must become as Rama, fighting great wars and traveling to the world's end for his wife and lover, pure devotion as the focus of life.

In the end, the ultimate truth or supreme knowledge, as it pertains to human life, is profoundly simple. And yet, paradoxically, it might be too sublime, too austere, too simple for us to easily fathom. It often dwells just beyond our grasp, although it is within us all the time. This truth has been sung by the mouths of countless mystics since time immemorial and was later embodied in the sacred texts and symbolism of many cultures and religions, but it has been mostly forgotten by modern man. This truth is not a concept, not a set of ideas, not a philosophical position—but a revealed knowledge of the bliss of unity, variously called "awakening," "illumination," "gnosis," or "enlightenment," whether reached through esoteric or spiritual practice, psychedelic substances, sex, or a multitude of other things. The method is inconsequential, the aim is the same. A life in quest of this truth leads to pilgrimage—to inner and outer journeys in a vigorous search for glimpses of truth that may be revealed to us, in us. And again, it is never somewhere else, but always "here," forever enshrined in the heart of hearts.

In the beginning of one's journey there might be the smaller goals of life one strives for—wealth, prosperity, success—which if and when attained, often lead to the realization that these smaller goals are but flickering, fleeting reflections of the true, ultimate goal. Sometimes great tragedy may also force us to confront this realization before we feel we are ready for it.

When I was by the river Ganga in Rishikesh, feeling dazed and other-worldly, plagued by my familiar entourage of inner demons, I partook in an evening puja. From a young boy I bought some incense and a little floating ghee lamp made out of leaves. I wrote something on a piece of paper—my ultimate wish and goal, the treasure I was seeking. I folded the little sheet of paper and slipped it, along with a coin, into the ghee lamp. Then I lighted it and watched in solemn silence as it drifted into the distance. It joined the stream of countless other floating lamps, becoming a small dot of light under the dark mountainous horizon, eventually vanishing completely into the night. That was several years ago now, and exactly what I scribed on the paper has been irretrievably lost to the sands of time. But the ultimate goal, the treasure I was seeking, is still there.

"Adinath Puri, when are you coming to India again, to the Kumbh Mela?" Surendra Puri asked me when we were about to part ways in Paris. I did not know what to answer. I felt that I had gone as far as I could on that particular path. But then again, you never know. As long as there is life, there is pilgrimage.

Even if I left all these things forever behind me, I do not believe they will ever leave me. The gifts I have received and the connections I have made will never be defiled. I will always treasure them as the talismans they are. As I am slumbering, somewhere in the distance I will hear bells ringing, calling me to them. And suddenly I will have a vision of the old warrior of the tales, who washed his bloody hands in a lake and rode triumphant over the mountains. I will remember all the blessings and bliss, the heights in which I have sung my will to the heavens, the wind carrying my voice into all directions. I will remember the valleys in which I have bled tears and blood of deep longing into the ground. And soon I am awake, standing on the edge again, an unknown breeze on my face.

We never got to drink whiskey by the river with Christian this time around to ruminate over days gone by as I had anticipated. But that is all just the past anyway. You can never drink whiskey at the same river twice. The river is ever flowing, marked by its sound, *sarasarasara*, invoking Saraswati, mother of creation and goddess of knowledge. And here in the present we did get to meet again. Seeing Surendra Puri and Christian felt familiar, like meeting brothers. Before we parted to go off into the night, I put my hand over Surendra's shoulder, and we hugged again. "We are family," or something to that effect, Surendra Puri said again. Perhaps it really is this simple, at least partially. Yoga means union, magic means connection. And this was it. We said our good-byes under the starry night sky of Paris. We would meet again.

As I wandered by the river, my heart was filled with a sense of yearning and a sense of everything happening simultaneously. Looking back at the time-worn images from my journeys forever carved into my soul, I was overcome with the beauty, tragedy, and majesty of those images. Sunrise, sunset. A starry night sky, the crashing waves of the ocean. A smile, a dance, an embrace. When we looked at each other, we saw ourselves. Creatures of consciousness in time, reflecting the infinite consciousness beyond time, connected to each other in the being of life, and what animates this being is the ultimate truth of the universe. Lost in moments such as these, the separation from the source and the angst of disconnection is lifted, the universe unveils itself in an act of joy, and the gods want to play. Suddenly, as the celestial seeks itself in the sensual, at the touch of a lover or in the arms of the great unknown, the divine discloses itself in unity and bliss.

Maybe I had found the long-sought-after darshan, the "beholding," after all.

> *All this (world) is conjured by magic;*
> *It is only the water of a desert mirage.*
> *Beyond all differences, beyond all forms,*
> *Truly, there is Shiva alone.*
> AHADHUT GITA, CHAPTER 7, VERSE 14

# 6
# FESTIVALS OF SPRING

*Transcendent manhood is the immanent cause of creation; transcendent womanhood is the efficient cause. There cannot be procreation without such union and there cannot be divine manifestation without their cosmic equivalent.*

SHIVA PURANA

IT WAS TWILIGHT AS WE, my new lover and I, wandered in the silent forest. Although it was spring, the snow still covered all things like a serene white shroud. We were on a path to a secluded place in the woods close to my home. I had visited that place for several years, albeit before in solitude. As we made our way through the forest, the sky turned dark, glistening with stars, and a sense of vastness overtook me, a feeling I remembered from my early childhood. And there we stood, under the northern constellations, our breath turning into frost in the cold night air. We were as trembling trees, our roots deep in the earth and our arms as branches reaching skyward.

One day later, that heartland in the north was very far away, as were the stars and silence. It was early morning and we were dodging rickshaws in the notorious Pahar Ganji area of Delhi, while a legless half man somehow shuffled past us on the street. Once again, I was among the chaos, the heat, and the unrelenting holy madness that is India. We walked up a narrow, run-down staircase to a restaurant on the rooftop of a house. Drinking beer and watching the dirty sunset over this seemingly hopeless city, something familiar came over me. I wondered what the hell I was doing here—again.

After my last journey in Hardwar during the Kumbh Mela festival, I thought I would never return. The unfolding of the events at the Mela had shown me a line in the sand that was not to be crossed. I had explored the Indian esoteric tradition of knowledge as far as I could and found both wisdom and folly; it had been a process of learning and unlearning. I had come to the conclusion that the esoteric path of India was not one to be embarked upon by a European such as me, who would ultimately remain a foreigner in its realms. At best, what could be found was a new way to see one's own hereditary spiritual landscape in the light of an ancient tradition. Drawing from these experiences and realizations, I had written a book that had recently been published in Finnish,* and I thought the story had come to an end.

Yet, divinely ironic as it was, here I was again. The story had come back to life. My fate seemed somehow entwined with this land and its ancient gods, with the figure of Shiva at the helm. However, this time it was not some forgotten god that had led me back to India, but my new lover, a student of yoga and ayurveda. Soon after meeting, we had found ourselves lying in natural hot springs on top of a mountain, sharing with each other our mantras, under the vast starry night sky. We had invoked each other, and now, our paths had crossed and become one.

As night fell, we headed to the Delhi train station. Our destination was Khajuraho, the remote temple town known throughout the world for its ancient erotic sculptures. As the train took off, a smiling Indian couple offered to share their dinner of rice, dal, and chapati with us. I climbed to the top bed of the three-tiered sleeper and sipped whiskey

---

*Pyhiinvaellus (Tallinn, Estonia: Salakirjat, 2013.)

from my flask, listening to the all-too-familiar sound of the train as it raced through the night. Like the mythic siren calls that lured sailors toward shipwrecks, this was the sound that always accompanied me during my travels, toward something beautiful perhaps, and dangerous certainly.

As the sun rose the next morning, we got into a small rickshaw and bounced along the country lanes, crossing fields lined with palm trees, eventually passing distant temples and rickety houses in the chilly morning air. I put an ochre-colored cloth around my lover's face and shoulders, as the sweet dew of dawn mixed with the smell of burning garbage. It was still early morning as we walked down the already bustling dirt road of the town. From a shoddy-looking seller on the street I bought a paperback called the *Kama Sutra,* which was not the ancient text so named. Obviously geared toward prurient sexual interest, it mostly contained erotic Indian art, along with prudish and unintentionally humorous descriptions. Based on the Kama Sutra, but retold here with much less finesse, it described various form of "congress" (sex), along with methods and advice on "striking, biting, and quarreling." For instance, it tells that for the sake of "mouth congress" (oral sex), courtesans abandon men of high value and become attached to "low persons, such as slaves and elephant drivers." Low persons, take note.

The erotic in all its forms, from profound to banal, seemed to underlie everything in Khajuraho. Vendors were selling souvenirs and art of an overwhelmingly amorous nature. We purchased an ornately carved wooden statue of a pair of hands against each other in the common blessing gesture, the *anjali* mudra. The hands could be opened up to reveal the secret inside: a couple having wild sex under a tree. All these things reflected the deeper meaning of the spring festival during which we had arrived in Khajuraho, by coincidence or destiny.

It was the culmination of the most auspicious of spring rites: Shivaratri, the great wedding night of lord Shiva and his lady of the mountains, Parvati. On this "Night of Shiva" Indians traditionally stay awake until dawn, participating in offerings to the lingam, phallus of Shiva, resting erect in the yoni of his consort. It is the sign of the universal man, Purusha, and represents the eternal renewal of life, divine reality, and the springing forth of the creative principle. The lingam is washed repeatedly with milk, yogurt, ghee, and honey water, while *datura* (thorn apple) or *bel* (wood apple) leaves are placed on it as offerings. Throughout the night, hordes of people crowd the temples—sadhus, Brahmins, householders, pilgrims, beggars—all devotees of Shiva. In endless repetitions they chant the Panchakshara, the five-syllable mantra:

## ॐ नमः शिवाय

*OM NA-MAH SHI-VA-YA*

This ancient festival of Shiva and the cult of the phallus is still echoed throughout the world in similar spring festivals, from Sumer to Greece, from Tibet to Europe. It still survives in the countless regional traditions, rites, festivities, and symbols of mankind. In alchemy it is known as Hieros Gamos, the sacred marriage. In pre-Christian northern Europe, the seat of the cult was located in Uppsala, Sweden, and was represented dominantly by a deity with a large phallus, identified as Frikko (commonly known as Frey) by Adam of Bremen. What is so deeply etched into the heart of man cannot be suppressed, and although it sometimes appears in more subtle, hidden forms, it still occupies a most central position in our world.

Close to the main temples of Khajuraho was the Shiv Sagar Tank (artificial lake) where devotees came for their ritual bath, especially during this particular night. The tank was surrounded by the hustle and bustle of a fair: camps, tents, street vendors, makeshift shrines, and rickety structures with flashy lights scattered throughout the landscape. The streets were crowded with wagons, cars, trucks, rickshaws, motorcycles and donkey carts, cows, dogs and monkeys, cripples, workers, families, school children, cops, sadhus, beggars, hecklers, tricksters, gawkers, snake handlers, sellers of everything and nothing, young guys with bleached jeans and cell phones, and the ever-present curious bystanders—in other words, the usual Indian crowd. It was a sweeping cross between a market, a religious gathering, and a carnival, with chaotic noises, honks, and carousel chimes surreally merging with devotional songs.

We circled the smaller, quieter Prem Sagar Lake nearby. At the edge of the water was a tiny shrine inside of which a goat was idly chewing on the offerings that had been left there. An old pipal tree rose through the paved ground, the stone images of the gods merging with its roots. In India, the tree itself is a living altar, decorated with bells, colored ribbons, trishuls, and *murtis* (images of the divine). The pipal tree (*Ficus religiosa*), also known as bodhi tree and recognizable by its heart-shaped leaves, is a sacred tree in all of India's native religions. It is under this tree that Shiva sits surrounded by his sages.

Another sacred tree, the *banyan* (*Ficus benghalensis*), with its thick vines touching the earth, strongly resembles the sadhu holy man with his matted jata locks reaching to the ground. People approach these and other trees for the blessings of their various spirits (i.e., particular personalities of nature). The banyan tree is said to embody the blessings of the *rishis* (the sages of the Vedas), deriving from *rish,* "to thrust." Rishis embody the spirit of procreation, which is why women tear off pieces of their saris and hang them on the tree when they wish to have a child.

I had seen pictures of Babas hanging from such trees, their brown and ash-gray limbs merging with the similarly colored trunks and branches. Seeing these striking images, I could not help but think of Allfather Odin, the high god of poetic wisdom and magic in the Nordic tradition. Odin "sacrificed himself to himself," and in a shamanic frenzy hung from the World Tree for nine nights in order to gain knowledge of the runes. The runes were more than mere letters; they were the ever-expansive secrets of the manifest world.

I was also reminded of what a Baba once told me: the original temples *were* sacred trees. A temple is something that is built where there is a signature of nature—a spring, a mountaintop, a grove, a tree. Before the edifice of man, these markers of nature were the first temples. This echoed the tradition of my native land of Finland as well as most of Europe, where sacred trees still feature prominently in folkways, stories, and customs (such as Jul, May Day, and midsummer), although many people have forgotten their deeper meaning. The trishul of Shiva and the tridentlike rune of Odin both mark the same thing: the cosmic World Tree itself, the axis mundi, connecting in a tripartite structure the celestial, earthly, and chthonic. This structure and principle are seen as existing in everything, including man himself (as the phallus), although he may have forgotten it. Certainly there were parallels between these ancient wild gods, who seemed to be drawing me into their realms toward the great secrets themselves.

Having made our oblations at the tree, we approached the structures of Khajuraho. At the gates we paid the "foreigners only" entrance fee and were frisked by uniformed officers. As we entered the grounds under the brilliant sun, stark silhouettes of ancient monuments stood before us like giants.

Built under the rule of the monarchs of the Chandela dynasty over a span of two hundred years, the temples of Khajuraho date back to the tenth century but are based on a tantric tradition dating back much farther into prehistory. Occupying eight square miles, the temples used to be surrounded by a high wall with eight gates marked by golden palm trees. As the Chandela dynasty fell, the temples fell with them. Gradually they were abandoned and forgotten, engulfed by the jungle and eventually covered by the sands of time. Of the original existing eighty temples, twenty-two remain. These remaining temples are now

Fig. 6.1. One of the Khajuraho temples
(Photograph by Justine Cederberg)

divided into three geographical groups: western, eastern, and southern. Out of all of them the western group hosts the largest and most impressive structures. Today, these are perhaps the most unique and famous of all the temples in India due to their detailed depictions of divine eroticism.

The sandstone temples are intricately carved with thousands upon thousands of overwhelming, timelessly beautiful and sensual sculptures. Creatures of the earth, the heavens, and the underworld, gods, men, and beasts all populate the edifices of the ancient monuments. Depicted are mythic animals such as Nandi, the bull of Shiva, and a boar incarnation of Vishnu, his surface covered with more than six hundred gods from the Indian pantheon. There are also scenes from worldly life: women applying makeup, nursing mothers, musicians, farmers, potters, and so on.

But the most dominant and striking among the various motifs present is that of copulation. Voluptuous, big-breasted, and heavy-hipped women fill the walls, fully decked out with ornate jewelry and little else. Nude damsels exhibit their well-formed backsides, while casting coy glances over their shoulders. Heavenly maidens seductively pose at every corner. Lovers embrace in ecstasy. Groups of three or more lovers engage in sex, while others watch from the side. Almost every possible sexual act between couples and groups (as well as some animals) is represented and repeated again and again. And of course, as throughout the rest of India, there are Shiva lingams standing erect everywhere.

However, the numerous portrayals of sex are not merely depictions of perversion run rampant, such as in the decline of ancient Rome. The Khajuraho monuments were built at the height of the culture that gave rise to them. True culture is the expression of the soul of the people who create it, and the monuments unveil what was at the core of religion for those people in ancient times: *maithuna,* sexual union in a ritual context. It seems like all the sculptures, even the ones engaged in more mundane activities, have paused for an eternal moment to witness the wedding of Shiva and Parvati—the cosmic union of the male

Fig. 6.2. Shiva Lingam, Khajuraho
(Photograph by Justine Cederberg)

and female. This union not only brings new creatures into life, but is a bridge between worlds of the temporal and of the timeless. It is the sacred marriage of earth and heaven.

Realizing that the experience of union represented by sacred sex is at the core of all life and that it is an expression of the undivided being variously called god, cosmic being, life force, and many number of other things, the ancient people who raised Khajuraho placed this understanding at the center of their worship. The temples pay tribute to the creative forces of the universe that lie at the root of life and are thus a remnant of a time when a more dynamic understanding of the world was still the prevalent norm of the day. They are an ode to purity, a poem set in stone, and represent the confluence of eroticism and religion yet untainted by later ideas of sin and separation.

It is in the light of the ecstasy, the passion, the mad abandon, and ultimately the union of the self with the other, which the copulating Shiva-Shakti represents, that other forms of so-called enlightenment pale in comparison. The temples are one of the last remaining bastions of this primeval knowledge, which has survived the destructive onslaught carried out in the name of later ideologies, namely Christianity and Islam. However, degeneration of this knowledge has also happened within modern so-called Hinduism, which has puritanically tried to whitewash the overtly erotic aspects of its mythos, such as Tantra and the worship of Shiva lingam, and reduce them into mere abstract symbols for something wholly different.

If an understanding of sacred sex as embodied in Khajuraho existed in another form in early esoteric Christianity, as has been claimed by various scholars and around which a whole genre of research exists, that understanding has been firmly lost by most modern-day religions and creeds. What was a central sacrament in primordial traditions has become taboo in currently prevailing religions. Instead of a direct experience of the mystery of god, approached through various ecstatic ritual practices such as sex, psychedelic sacraments, or ordeals, what we have left are various degenerate priest classes and written dogmas to act as intermediary forces between us and the sacred we seek.

A refined understanding of sexual ecstasy, as carved in the sculptures of Khajuraho, has been displaced. What is essentially joyous, vital, and an affirmation of the life principle has been inverted into something vile, sin tainted, or abstract and symbolic or has been reduced to mere physical action. The various modern-day apologetic interpretations of the supposed "meanings" of the Khajuraho temple art, which manage to stand directly in opposition to its apparent nature, are forever removed from the direct truths that the art embodies. In such a conflict the concrete and the abstract are forever poised against one another.

It comes as no surprise then that this motif of a celebration of divine union was not well received by the British of the Victorian era. The deserted and overgrown temple complex was rediscovered in the early 1800s by an officer in the British Army, who declared their workmanship "beautifully and exquisitely carved," but their subject matter "extremely indecent and offensive." That a religious celebration and joyous ode to the principle at the root of all life could be considered offensive tells volumes about the degenerate mentality of that era.

Despite the ever-present tension at religious festivals in India caused by looming threats—crowds running amok and violent eruptions, but primarily terrorist attacks—on this night of Shiva, something was different. The lines to the main Shiva temple were like throbbing serpents, the crowds large and rowdy, but the spring air was full of revelry. In the midday heat, we strolled across the grassy fields from one temple to another, pausing to lie down on the grassy fields outside of them. In the shade of the ancient seductive statues we took sips of whiskey, embraced, and kissed. Doors that were normally closed now seemed to all be open for us. Security guards at the temples welcomed us warmly with loud shouts

Fig. 6.3. Heavenly maidens inside one of the temples of Khajuraho
(Photograph by Justine Cederberg)

of "Shiva Parvati!" Maybe they saw us as an auspicious sign, reminding them of the divine couple of Shiva and his consort Parvati, known to take many forms—some of them surprising and strange.

Slowly the day turned into twilight, the hour of Shiva, and the temples were being closed up for the night. In this liminal hour, we approached the loftiest of the temples, the Kandariya Mahadeva mandir. This temple is built to resemble Mount Kailash in the Himalayas, the abode of Lord Shiva, with its highest peak spire, *sikhara*, rising to nearly 102 feet, surrounded by eighty-four smaller spires or *urushringas*. Eight hundred sculptures are carved on its interior and exterior walls. The interior of the temple resembles a cave. As we entered the temple grounds, a guard greeted us with the already familiar shout "Shiva Parvati!" He then led us into the inner chamber, the *garbha-griha,* where a marble Shiva lingam stood in the dark. "Now you sit down and pray," the guard said, and left us to rush all other visitors out of the temple.

As we sat in the darkness, the sounds from outside became distant. The ancient stone edifice had darkened with age to the degree that it was hard to even see the ceiling of the cave-like room. The place resonated with the infinite number of invocations conducted here during the course of the ages. I closed my eyes and thought of Shiva in his form of a column of fire without beginning or end. Instantly, my consciousness expanded like a pillar into space.

Outside the sun was setting. The temple walls, covered with countless couples forever making love, were gleaming in gold and red.

Leaving the temple grounds, we climbed to the top of a nearby treehouse and watched the ancient monuments being lit up against the darkness by colored lights. As the lights illuminated the temples, so was this night of Shiva illuminated by the presence of something strong and primal. The celebrations were reaching their peak and there was electricity in the air. We walked through the bustling streets and returned to our guesthouse, where we could look across a field to the fair beyond.

Incense smoke filled the sweltering air as our shadows moved across the high walls of our room. We had transformed the typically decrepit guesthouse, which had cracks in the walls and electric wiring hanging out here and there, into a makeshift temple. A wooden cabinet served as a shrine with candles, flowers, and cups filled to the brim with whiskey and a potent aphrodisiac plant. A large old mirror leaned against the wall, and our bed stood in the center of the room. In the distance, we could hear a constant cacophony of clinging bells and wild chanting and shouting.

As echoes of devotion filled the night air, my lover and I worshipped the gods in a more direct way. Rather than seeking effigies of stone, we beheld the divine in each other through the sacrament of sex. It was a rite of spring—violent beauty in a blissful union of opposites. My lover's sweat tasted sweet, as her face blurred and turned into that of some primal goddess. In the mirror we saw our reflection and here at the flowing confluence of two streams, the sexual and spiritual, we *were* the gods incarnate, the divine couple made flesh.

Finally, exhausted and spent, we drifted into dreams, the night still inhabited by Shiva's troupe of ghouls, spirits, and beasts—all the wild, untamed forces and personalities of nature.

The next morning, in the afterglow of the night before, we cycled through the quiet countryside, through nearby villages and fields, passing temples and little pastel-hued shacks and dodging calm Hindu cows here and there. We crossed a river where women were doing laundry while carefree children played on its banks around a little Shiva lingam. Eventually we arrived at the eastern group of temples, located slightly outside the Khajuraho center. They were smaller than the ones we had seen the day before, but clearly featured the same motifs. On a field by an Adinath temple,* hundreds of broken erotic statues

*In this case, Adinath, the name I was given in initiation, refers to the founder of Jainism in addition to the "First Lord" Shiva.

lay scattered, fragments embodying a perhaps forgotten knowledge.

At dusk we returned to the center of the town for a final visit to the oldest still-functioning temple of the Khajuraho structures, the Matangeshwarmandir. Dating from circa 900 CE, this old temple is so revered that Khajuraho is still sometimes called the City of Matangeshwar. Entering the temple grounds, we could see it gleaming in the distance, its entrance marked by colorful flags.

We followed the winding path to the ancient temple. A persistent huckster selling something or other followed us despite our determination to ignore him, but finally he stopped by a large tree growing right by a long staircase ascending to the sacred structure. We climbed its worn stone stairs and, touching the ground of the threshold and then our foreheads, entered through its gates. Before us stood a giant Shiva lingam, its height and circumference literally filling the entire temple. The lingam invoked sublime nobility and awe, its imposing presence a sign of the power that it embodied. And there, on that closing holy night of Shiva, I offered my story, my book, as a gift to the gods. The presiding Brahmin priest smiled and carefully laid the book at the root of the stony colossus. As we wandered down the stairs and into the night, something had come full circle. The story had returned to its source.

When we returned home in a few weeks, it would be Easter. Named after an ancient goddess of dawn, the age-old spring festival filled with rabbits and eggs marked when the first green would be sprouting forth through the barren winter earth, signifying the Eternal return, both in nature and within man himself. In the forest, the snow would have finally begun to melt.

# 7
# EARTH TURNS INTO GOLD

*Behind your thoughts and feelings, my brother, there stands
a mighty ruler, an unknown sage—whose name is self. In
your body he dwells; he is your body. There is more reason
in your body than in your deepest philosophy.*

FRIEDRICH NIETZSCHE,
*THUS SPOKE ZARATHUSTRA*

HANUMAN, THE FAMOUS MONKEY GOD, stood before us in
the temple courtyard as a bright orange statue that seemed to glow in
contrast to the dark sky. We sat down by its feet. It was the night before
we would leave Khajuraho.

"I do Hanuman puja for you," said the young priest who had waved
us over. He tied red and orange cords around our wrists, marked our
third eyes with colored paste, and started reciting seemingly endless
mantras.

As the pages turned and the mantras rolled on, my mind drifted
to years back. In the *Ramayana* there is a tale of how Hanuman, devotee of Rama, helped fight the demon king Ravana and free Rama's captured wife, Sita. The brother of Rama, Lakshman, had been slain and
Rama's army of monkeys was discouraged. It was up to Hanuman to fly

to the Himalayas before sunrise to collect the herb that would restore Lakshman to life. When he arrived, Hanuman discovered he had forgotten which plant to collect—he was, after all, a monkey. He was also running out of time. In this dire situation, Hanuman gathered all his strength, uprooted the entire mountain, and snatched the sun under his arm to prevent it from rising. Then he returned triumphant. This tale is reenacted annually during the Dussehra festival and given form in the popular image of Hanuman flying through the air carrying a mountain and a sun disk.

I had attended the Dusshera festival many years ago in Delhi on my first travels in India. During the festival huge effigies of Ravana filled with explosives were blown up amid the crowds in a chaotic spectacle. It was theater approximating ritual, and ritual approximating mythic reality, but at the time, I did not yet fully understand what it meant.

I was roused from my mythic reflections as the priest cut short his recital of mantras. He blessed us, and sure enough, gave me a high price tag for the puja. I gave him some rupees, a small fraction of what he asked for, and we got up to leave. No matter how seemingly benevolent an action may be, everything in India came with a price—*especially* blessings.

At dusk the next day we approached the train-station parking lot, where for reasons unknown to us, rickshaw drivers were beating each other up with long canes. We hurried through the crowd and caught the train. A short while later, the train creaked and departed from the Khajuraho station. I looked through the barred window at the darkening landscapes. We were headed south, toward Kerala, at the end of the Indian subcontinent. As the vistas grew darker outside, I wondered where the story would lead me from here on out. Not mere fiction, the story had been written with my lifeblood and was entwined with my destiny. Now, as it had seemingly reached some kind of culmination, I was both empty and full. I could sense that there was a shift happening but could not yet put my finger on it.

After a long journey, we arrived on the island of Fort Kochi. On a sandy beach littered with plastic garbage, we watched large fishing nets hovering over murky waters against a gray-gold sunset. Later, I sat wearily on the balcony of our oppressively hot room in a touristy area, overlooking the street below, busy with travelers and the shops and the hawkers that catered to them, which after enough traveling all starts to look alike. The next evening, having moved to a quieter area, I watched as goats walked down the street outside our guesthouse, while dark clouds gathered. A little later, rain poured down in torrents.

As the streets filled with water, I was flooded with waves of a strange malaise. Something finally caught up with me then, and for several days I was ill with sudden peaks of high temperature and low mood. Feverish dreams grew into violently intense creatures, devourers that would arrive at night and cast their shadow over me well into the next day. In one dream I was lying naked on an mountain of human bones, while another one was full of rape and horrible violence. Some dreams would echo themselves in the waking world, such as in a bit of random disquieting news about an Austrian couple having been beaten and gang raped while bike riding somewhere in India. But the most crushing dream by far was one in which I was confronted by someone I myself had caused deep suffering. These dreams haunted me and knew how to tear open the deepest wounds. Their liminal presence would cause tears to well up, and daylight would not completely banish them.

In Greek mythology, there are two kinds of dreams: false and essentially meaningless dreams that come through a gate of ivory and true and prophetic dreams that arrive through a gate of horn. Perhaps something in my depths was calling to be heard. I realized that like the visionary dreams that had guided me in life before, these dreams were showing me something, revealing an underlying truth—no matter how painful or how unwilling I was to accept it. The only way out from these nightmarish landscapes was inevitably *through* them.

My spirit was uplifted as we attended a demonstration of *kalaripayat,* the ancient martial art of Kerala. Sometimes called the "mother of martial arts," it is considered one of the oldest of such traditions in the world, and some trace it as far back as 900 BCE. According to myth, it was founded by the sixth avatar (incarnation) of Vishnu, Parashurama, descendant of Brahma and disciple of Shiva. It was Shiva himself who taught the martial arts to Parashurama, whose name literally means "Rama with axe." With the advent of firearms and modern warfare, kalaripayat went into decline and had to be practiced in secret as it was banned by the British. The art was partially rediscovered in the twentieth century, but it still remains highly esoteric and local.

Kalaripayat includes unarmed combat techniques, such as striking, kicking, and grappling, as well as the use of a myriad of traditional (and antiquated) weapons like swords and shields. Also essential to the art are meditation and methods of healing, including massage and the use of oils and herbs. Kalaripayat styles vary by locale and can be roughly divided into the northern, central, and southern styles. Southern styles are practiced in the open air, while northern styles (distinguished by their emphasis on weapons) are practiced in a *kalari,* a training hall resembling a shrine. Kalaris are commonly built below ground level and made of soft clay in order to prevent injuries resulting from practice. In every kalari there is a *puttara,* a seven-tiered shrine in the southwest corner where the guardian deity presides, often an avatar of Shiva or the goddess called Bhagavathi in the Kerala, Goa, and Maharashtra regions. Every morning before practice, the martial artists offer flowers, water, and incense to the presiding deity. The kalari is thus more than a mere training hall—it is also a temple. The same can be said of kalaripayat itself: as a whole, it is more than a series of fighting techniques; it is a spiritual martial-art tradition.

The demonstration of kalaripayat was presented by a Brahmin priest and performed by four men in their thirties from local families of fishermen. They were dressed in simple black loincloths tied with dark red strips of fabric (see color plate 11). The performance included striking and grappling techniques, as well as weapons demonstrations, the most impressive of which was a long whip made out of sharp pieces of razor blade, which could be concealed around the waist like a belt, to be unleashed in an instant.

However, more impressive than the weapons or the techniques were the martial artists themselves. As I watched them move, a reminder of sublime, warlike beauty came over me, such as I had seen before embodied in some boxers. The martial artists embodied human balance and strength, even though they had visible flaws that might make them handicapped or seriously disadvantaged under other circumstances. One of them was unusually short. Another one, a tall, fit, mustachioed man, had suffered from polio as a child and had been told he would never walk properly. His left leg was seriously misshapen and twisted to one side from his ankle. But as I watched these men spar, spin through the air, or take on statuesque postures, it was obvious that they had not let their limitations or pain define them. The Brahmin priest told us that they, not having a training hall to practice in anymore, now trained every morning on a rooftop under the sun.

After the presentation, the four men hung out in the back, smiling and chatting with a few curious people, a calm air about them. The mustachioed man was smoking a cigarette. It was as if that they had something that could not be taken away from them, an inner resolve that made them seem untouchable. In their demonstration of kalaripayat, I glimpsed something of the vitality that I had often found lacking in the more esoteric world of yoga as I had experienced it. There was no grand temple, merely a rooftop under the sun. There were no coughing, skinny sadhus or potbellied gurus, merely four healthy, able-bodied fishermen. There were no claims to grand titles, lineages, or hierarchies, only movement and the embodiment of spirit and strength.

We soon left Fort Kochi behind. On our way toward the high peaks of the mountain region of Munnar, we visited an ayurvedic garden where a local man, a self-declared Christian, showed us the plethora of plant life. I wandered through the garden, still weary from the illness and not eating properly, watching gentle patches of melancholic fog settle across the mountains. As we were leaving, the man said, "Know nature, and you will know god."

In the mountains, our guesthouse was situated on a high ledge with views over the surrounding valleys. Early in the morning, we started hiking to the peak of the mountain along the slope on which we stayed. Shiva Shankara in his form as lord of the mountains, Girisha, seemed to loom over us. Datura, Shiva's sacred plant used as a hallucinogen and a poison, grew everywhere. The beautiful plant, also known as angel's trumpet or moonflower, was favored by the locals for attempted suicides.

I made oblations by a small cave-like Shiva altar set in stone at the root of the mountain, recognizable by Shiva's symbols: the trishul and the three lines of ash. We climbed up the steep path, rising above the tree line and eventually beyond paths altogether. Close to the summit I sat down on a big rock overlooking the mountains. All was silent under the scorching sun and boundless blue sky. The ordinary world of men below seemed distant. Even my ordinary self seemed somewhere far away, as the dreams that had followed me grew more quiet and every-day thoughts faded.

It is no accident that Shiva is venerated in forests and caves and especially on mountaintops, well beyond the confines of ordinary life and people. Divinity dwells outside the borders of civilization, beyond the manmade, and can be approached in the solitude and sacrality of nature. All alone with oneself, stripped of the protective falsehoods and arbitrary identities that characterize much of modern life, true being can begin to reveal itself.

Fig. 7.1. The mountains of Munnar, Kerala
(Photograph by Justine Cederberg)

In these heights we took respite from the rest of the world for a few days. In the evening, there were silent countryside lanes, cloudy sunsets over the tea plantations, and random lightning strikes that illuminated the pitch-black night for freeze-frame instances, thunder echoing in the distance. On the TV, Indian soap operas with ancient gods played by bad actors.

As we descended from the heights to the plains, the bus swayed dangerously down winding dirt roads. The mountain air felt fresh on my face as we raced through the valleys, fields, and villages. Still, a gnawing sense of malaise hovered over me—I was still not well and an uneasiness left by my dreams persisted.

In the jungle of Periyar, we stayed in a little shack at the edge of a vast forest. Beyond a little wall was the deep jungle and the boars, water buffalos, monkeys, lizards, tigers, and other beasts that inhabited it, some of which would visit our shack in the morning. Walking in the jungle, we encountered wild elephants down by a stream and quietly watched them bathe, their dark skin glistening in the evening sun. Later, riding on the back of such a noble giant, I felt the massive, elemental creature rocking under me.

Ganesh, the elephant-headed son of Shiva, was the remover of obstacles, and I silently called on him to remove whatever was stifling my spirit. In the human body, the seat of Ganesh is thought to be the *muladhara* chakra (the first or root chakra, seat of kundalini energy), reputedly located at the base of the spinal column. Ganesh is considered to be the body and earth, the source of sexuality and primal power. And yet, even though elephants are considered divine in the form of Ganesh, they are sadly an object of rampant poaching, capture, and cruelty. They are on the list of endangered species, as their population has been in a steady decline caused by habitat loss, degradation, and fragmentation, which in turn are the result of an expanding human population and industrial development. It is a tragic irony that a natural creature is revered in an abstract "spiritual" form, while often disregarded in material reality.

This kind of distancing from reality is symptomatic of much of the so-called spiritual world, where high-minded concepts reign over harsh realities. Nature is romanticized beyond recognition and turned into a thoroughly benevolent, nurturing mother. In reality the mother is not merely the womb of life but also the tomb of death. In stark contrast, the attitude toward nature of rural pagans of old, who were forced to deal with the constant struggle for mere survival, was surely much different from the urban tree huggers of today. Beyond the protective walls of cities and modern comforts, one quickly realizes that while nature provides nourishment and life, it is also harsh, cruel, and fairly indifferent toward individual living beings. If one truly wants to "know god through nature," one must recognize nature in all its radiant beauty *and* its harrowing brutality. The newborn sucks life from its mothers breast as the lion strikes down its prey. The serpent swallows its tail, as all life feeds on other life.

Late in the evening, under the dark sky over the jungle, my thoughts turned to Kali, the black goddess of destruction, whose dark body is the night sky itself. Kali is the bloodthirsty, blood-drunk one, gorging herself on death and destruction with an all-consuming appetite. But Kali is also the destroyer of illusions, especially illusions we might have about ourselves and our own finite nature. And she is time, all producing, all consuming, as everything that is created in time will inevitably be consumed by time as well. Approaching this paradox, turning to Mother Kali means embracing both of the intertwined forces of the universe of which all life and death consists: the creative and the destructive.

A few days later, consideration of the harshness of nature faded away as nature once again appeared gentle and benevolent in the form of the goddess Parvati, while we peacefully floated through the Keralan backwaters in a rented houseboat. I drank beer, and my partner lay in the sun, as the captain steered our vessel along the canals. Occasional goats and children stared idly at us on the shore. In the evening, again under a starry sky, we sat on deck and listened to the sounds from a small village nearby, where people were having their evening meals in candlelight, talking and laughing. We fell asleep to the lull of the water and soft buzz of the jungle.

Moving south, we eventually arrived at our final destination of Varkala, contrasting high, menacing cliffs and long, soft beaches with views over the Arabian Sea. The scenery was paradisiacal. Looking over the edge of the high cliffs down to the waves beating violently on the rocks, I could not help but think it would be an ideal place for a dramatic, classic film death. In the evening, we marveled at the natural poetry of the flaming sun disk sinking into the ocean. But despite the sublime scenery, Varkala was no paradise. In contrast to the natural serenity of the location and its age-old sacred sites, Varkala, as other such paradisiacal places in India, has unfortunately not escaped the intrusive commercialism directed at tourists. The main beach cliffside is lined with endless stalls run by aggressive shopkeepers selling glass pipes and garish T-shirts, while cafés blare techno, rock, and reggae music appealing to the tourists tastes—or lack thereof. Smirky, supposedly enlightened Western hippies with dreadlocks and baggy pants wander around aimlessly, casting stoned stares into the sea.

We settled in a hut on the seashore at a distance from the more touristy area. On our first morning, I awoke from my still-anxious dreams to the sound of a murder of crows. But like the birds, my dreams soon drifted away with the wind, as I lay in the pool surrounded by softly swinging palm trees, staring out over the ocean.

The cliffsides were laden with striking rough-hewn stone staircases and little natural streams trickling down from somewhere inside the rocks. Like the mythic fountains of youth, some of these streams were said to have healing, restorative powers, and they were often visited by the locals who would perform oblations at them. We wandered along the site of one such fountain, the Papanasam Beach. *Papanasam* translates to the "destroyer of sins." As the name suggests, there is a belief that swimming there washes away the transgressions of one's life. While I am certainly no believer in sin, the warm and violent waves washed over me regardless, finally cleansing me of some of the heaviness that had accompanied me, as did the scorching sun. Slowly, I could feel my strength returning.

We walked to the end of the beach and found it was not just any sandy shore but an actual cremation ground where human ashes were dispersed in the currents of the sea. In the shade of a small restaurant we took in the bittersweet air of this strange meeting place of devout mourners, priests, fishermen, and sunbathers flanked by a large upscale hotel. It was joy and sorrow walking hand in hand, people swimming in waters where human ashes interspersed, life and death merging and flowing together.

As part of a local spring festival, huge crowds gathered in the streets of central Varkala. Dancers performed traditional, ritualistic dances to the accompaniment of pounding drums. In the temple grounds, people were queueing to get the blessings from this or that god. As fireworks went off, a procession of elephants decorated in colorful armors and flower garlands walked through the crowds. I had heard it was not uncommon for such elephants to go berserk and run through the gathered masses, and this scenario did not seem all that unlikely. Later in the evening, trucks with enormous plastic gods rigged on top of them drove through the streets, accompanied by a bombastic cacophony of music and narration. Actors dressed up as different divinities intermingled with the crowds. An actor playing Ardhanarishvara, Shiva in his hermaphroditic form, gave me a flirty wink.

Through all of these events, set against an ostensibly tropical paradise, a strange mood sometimes overtook me. Gazing over the raging sea, I sensed a storm within. Perhaps I was getting tired of wandering.

Throughout all my journeys I had come to realize that one does not ever arrive anywhere, nor does one escape anything either. "The mind is a place of its own," wrote John Milton, "and in itself can make a heaven of hell, a hell of heaven." Once one has visited enough temples, they eventually all start looking alike. The novelty wears off and things appear as a mere facade, as the sounds and colors of festivals turn into noise. I was growing tired of the seemingly endless search for some exotic treasure at the end of the rainbow. That had never been my search to begin with, as I had sensed that the treasure, whatever it was, was already inside, and that whatever I found in the outer world would simply reflect this. Yet I sometimes felt like the monkey god Hanuman, who leapt through the air, reaching for the sun, mistaking it for a fruit.

As the waves kept crashing endlessly into the rocks of the cliffs, my mind wandered to something that happened many years ago on a similar beach. I had been swimming, and as I walked up from the water, I saw a lone black dog sitting on the shore waiting for me. As I sat down, the dog came over, took his place at my feet, and remained there for the rest of the day. As the sun started setting, I took my leave and wandered along the shoreline. The black dog followed and for a long while we walked together. Suddenly, as we got close to the guesthouse I was staying at, the black dog was attacked by a feral pack. They barked and snarled, rending and biting, many against one, but the black dog fought back and survived. As I watched him run off into the sunset, I thought once more of Shiva, who is said to ride a black dog or take its form as the frightful and fierce Bhairava.

The color of Bhairava is black, representing enigma. Devotion to Bhairava can be shown by feeding and taking care of dogs, associated as they are with wandering ascetics and Dattatreya, who himself is often accompanied by four strays. By their nature, dogs are both violent and devotional. Like Shiva, dogs are outsiders, marginal creatures who move at the edges, associated more with wilderness than with civilization. They often haunt cremation grounds, and it has been said that when a black dog eats a corpse, it can be thought of as Shiva freeing its soul.

In Kathmandu, Nepal, I had encountered Bhairava as a stone sculpture towering thirteen feet high on Durbar Square. Animal sacrifices are made at his feet each year. His temple in Varanasi, the Kal Bhariav Mandir, had bloodred walls. In Hardwar I had my great bath in the Ganga at a place bearing his name, the Bhairava Ghat. Throughout India, in some of his temples, alcohol (usually thought of as a *tamasic* substance and not generally part of Hindu ritual) is given as an offering to please the deity. As a side note, an Indian newspaper recently reported that at one such Bhairava temple a large quantity of alcohol that had been given to the priests had "mysteriously" gone missing—quite the riddle indeed.

Because I was connected to Shiva Bhairava, I saw myself in that lone black dog. For reasons perhaps not entirely known to me, my spirit resonated with the night side, with enigmas well beyond the norm. While I sought to reach soaring heights, dark and violent things lay in my depths. Striving for ascension distanced me farther from the plain where most people resided. For me the way of Shiva had been a solitary one, as the image of the lone Shiva Shankara sitting in the mountains depicted. I also realized that the things I sought might be ultimately unreachable in this world. And here lay a paradox: a spirit that set me aside from ordinary people. As expressed by countless sages, artists, and madmen throughout history, men of such spirit will find no home in a banal world but will seek it on mountaintops and far shores and beyond paths well-traveled. Perhaps this meant that I would always be at odds with society in some way or perhaps remain a stranger in its midst.

Yet as I persisted on the path and endured the inevitable opposition and conflict, eventually something subtle began to reveal itself. At the darkest night of the soul, I turned ever inward. And there, in the core of my being, something radiant lay hidden. As the sun reveals itself from behind a thick covering of clouds, so in sudden moments did the sun within bring forth its illumination. Was this sun the eternal, undivided self that the sages spoke of, already in union with the all? Was it *sat-cit-ananda*—"being, consciousness, bliss"—an experience of pure consciousness and ultimate reality? Either way, these bursts of radiance gave me the trust to seek within myself that being who would act as a guide for me and embrace the seemingly innate conflicts of the world.

As on many other beachfronts of India, littered along the coast of Varkala there are countless yogic retreats, ayurvedic centers, and classes for inner peace, harmony, and tranquillity. But I did not crave any of these things. I did not crave peace. There was something sedate and vacuous about all of it. "Where there is peace, the warlike man attacks himself," wrote Nietzsche. I longed for something vital and forceful, something pure. Many seekers are by nature drawn by either the mystical, internal path or the martial, outer path, whereas I sought the place where the two intersected. I felt I was poised between things and under me was an abyss of existential nihilism that had to be overcome time and again through perpetual spiritual warfare. I felt something stirring in my soul—a violent current. I cared not so much about rightness and rationality; I wanted to burn and burn brightly, and if necessary, be consumed by the great flame itself. I was a romantic in that way.

In light of this inner stirring, I thought again of the fishermen I had seen practicing kalaripayat. They seemed to embody something wholly lacking on the so-called mystical paths so prevalent everywhere in the modern world—an immediacy of values. I wanted to seek out practitioners of kalaripayat in Varkala, so I asked the locals if they knew of any or of a kalari, but no one seemed to know of either. After a long search, we bumped into someone who knew about such a place in the area, and one evening we walked down narrow lanes and alleys in search of the place, following vague, confusing instructions. When we finally found it we discovered it was called, not surprisingly, Shiva Garden. In the backyard we met Jayan, a practitioner of kalaripayat. He was slightly surprised to meet a Westerner seeking knowledge about the local martial art, and we sat down to talk. Jayan offered us tea and shared with us his insights as a practitioner in a low, almost hushed voice. There was an air of humility and quietness about him, not uncommon among those accustomed to rigorous training in a martial art. A lone punching bag hung on a nearby tree.

"Do you know Shiva?" was one of the first things Jayan asked me. Yes, I did know. He continued, "Shiva's dance comes from the tradition of kalaripayat." The image of Shiva as Nataraja, the cosmic dancer, held the key to many seeming paradoxes. Like the divine hermaphrodite in alchemy and the hermetic tradition of the West, or the occult image of the Baphomet, Shiva is portrayed as both male and female, symbolizing the *coniunctio oppositorum,* the union of opposites. Shiva dances the *ānandatāndava,* the seventh and last of his dances, which brings together all aspects of his being. His ecstatic dance in an arc of fire reflects the eternal ebb and flow of the universe revealing and concealing itself in a cycle of creation-destruction-renewal.

Shiva's head is decorated by a skull held there by two serpents, marking unavoidable death. Being the lord of expansive consciousness and all intoxicating substances, Shiva's flowing hair is woven with the highly poisonous and psychedelic datura blossoms. Shiva's four arms mark the four-fold, cyclical nature of manifestation and time, as well as the cardinal directions. His lower left hand is in the *gajahasta* mudra and points to his left foot, which is raised as if floating in the air—attaining liberation, movement becomes light. In his upper left hand he holds a flame that burns away the veils of illusion. With his right leg he tramples on a demon dwarf, *Apasmāra-purusa,* representing the "small self" of ignorance, while his right hand holds the hourglass-shaped damaru drum, marking time with its rhythm. Finally, he makes the gesture of an open hand, palm facing outward, the *abhaya* mudra, dispelling fear and offering divine protection and bliss to those who approach him.

Before I knew of any of these mythic connotations, Shiva in his form as the cosmic dancer had become familiar to me. Long before ever considering traveling to India, I had bought a statue of Shiva in this very depiction. The image had resonated with me, although I did not then fully grasp its meaning. Later, the very same image of Shiva was on the first half a blotter of LSD I ever took. Like a self-fulfilling prophecy, my experience of LSD was in line with the image of the dancing god himself: it was a release from fear and a glimpse into the nature of pure consciousness. That I would much later receive one of Shiva's names, Adinath Puri, for myself in an initiation was another affirmation of my connection to this ancient god.

Making parallels between the movement of Shiva in his dance and that of a kalaripayat practitioner, Jayan described kalaripayat as an esoteric, spiritual discipline. Understood in this light, the combination of movement, training, and sparring becomes a form of "active meditation" in the temple of the body. As in other martial arts, when one is surrounded by ceaseless conflict, eventually an inner silence takes over. The lessons learned in the ring or in combat can be applied to every situation in life outside of them. It is an inner alchemy, where, through strife, base matter is transformed into gold.

Some people have expressed worry that kalaripayat is a "dying tradition," but Jayan refuted this outright. "The tradition of kalaripayat is not interested in seeking students or being popular. It is not for everyone. It works the other way around: the student has to seek kalaripayat. And the student has to find and convince a master that they are *worthy* of becoming students. Otherwise it is a waste of time." Training in kalaripayat meant committing to personal transformation within its context, and that was a lifetime effort, not a hobby or skill set or weekend retreat.

When speaking of these masters and gurus of kalaripayat, the *gurukkal,* Jayan became visibly excited, and his otherwise hushed tone rose slightly. His descriptions of the gurukkal were surrounded by a mythic aura, like that attributed to magicians, shamans, or sadhus. He told me about an accomplished master, a fiercely independent wild man, who allegedly had a great capacity to heal people. Jayan described him as "a crazy guy, climbing trees upside down, feet first!"

Be that as it may, from what I had learned one should not await for miracles or masters, but simply go to work on oneself, as everything one wants to become is already there, hidden within. "God helps those who help themselves," as the old saying goes. There is not just one answer to all the questions, and there are many diverse paths that lead to the same clearing in the woods of the spirit. Different personalities and polarities require different approaches, but if the aim is the restoration of balance, everyone can and should strive to make an effort.

Much of what Jayan said resonated with me. As in many other areas, although we have our own traditions of martial arts in the West, we mostly lack the more spiritual or mythic aspects of them and therefore often turn to and mythologize the Eastern martial arts. We are trained how to fight, but not how to heal or how to restore balance and apply our knowledge outside of conflict. Equally, what the Eastern martial arts have in terms of myths and traditional holistic systems, they perhaps lack in outright pragmatism and simplicity.

To counter the intensive stirrings inside of me, which would at times threaten to be all-consuming, I had also sought the sun in the outer world, in the wisdom of the flesh. I had started training in the Western martial art of boxing only a few years ago but had become intensely familiar with the world that it had opened for me. As a naturally peaceful, contemplative person, I had realized that thinking and cerebral disciplines only get you to a certain point. I had started to loathe the "pale intellectual," the "weary philosopher." Fighting had heralded a dawning of a new kind of knowing, a new kind of wisdom, one not rooted in words but in pulsing, red-hot blood. Perpetual conflict brings sublime tranquility. There is a deep serenity that descends upon the practitioner after an intense session of training and especially sparring. Sanctity takes a seat in aching, sweating flesh. For me, it was a redemption from the tiredness of life. For a moment, all transgressions are forgiven, all confusion laid aside, and there is only simple, pure being.

I related this to Jayan, and his response was simple: "Any experience can be turned spiritual." I thanked him for his time, and we walked into the night, toward the sea roaring in the distance.

In the next few days, we moved even farther away from the hustle and bustle of the more popular spots to a silent little place by a beach where the local fishermen set out in their boats in the morning and lay their nets out to dry in the afternoon. As the surroundings grew simpler and more silent, so did I. The sea and sun were cleansing me, mirroring the sun within and the sea in my veins.

My thoughts turned again to Hanuman, the monkey god. In the legends and stories, Hanuman is the epic hero. He is the son of the Lord of Wind, Vāyu, and his guru is the Sun. Sometimes Hanuman is perceived as an avatar of Shiva. Whereas Vishnu can be seen as a transcendent, perhaps unreachable divinity, Hanuman represents the *means* for reaching this divinity. Hanuman is the embodiment of a virtuous human life, characterized by *shakti* and *bhakti*—strength and devotion. Sometimes he is not the smartest of beings, but his devotion is what gets him through in the end. He is called Mahavir, "the great courageous," while another name for him is Bajrang Bali, "the strong one who is saffron colored."

Hanuman was not only loved by millions of Hindus but also centrally revered by practitioners of traditional martial arts, in particular wrestlers, who occupy a sacred position in northern India, having become embodiments of a national ideal based on a discipline of the body. These wrestlers are distinct from, but in several ways comparable to, the sannyasis. The word *akhara* itself (as in Juna Akhara of the Naga Babas), meaning a "martial or monastic order and their place of practice," originally referred to a wrestling ring or a gymnasium where martial arts were practiced. As such, the akhara represents "a shrine of strength where earth is turned into gold."* Both the practitioners of kalaripayat and the wrestlers were living representations of this process; both worshipped at the shrines of strength, both embraced friction in order to create gold.

And so it was that I began to finally realize what Hanuman embodied and what his stories were about. Over time, my focus had shifted from the symbolic to the concrete, from the monastic to the martial, from the internal to the external. After wandering in dark mystic mazes, I had raised my gaze upward. And as Hanuman, I had made the Sun my guru. I had sought for not only the confluence of sex and religion, but of art and action, of contemplation and conquest. Having grown weary of unnecessarily complicated, obtuse esoteric systems, I longed to return to the simple, immediate values that the Sun communicates. I longed for radiant open temples under the naked sky surrounded by tall, trembling trees. And finally, I longed not for everlasting journeys, but for home.

---

*Joseph S. Alter, *The Wrestler's Body: Identity and Ideology in Northern India* (Berkeley: University of California Press, 1992), 26.

# 8
# A WOLF AGE

*Brothers will fight and kill each other,*
*sisters' children will defile kinship.*
*It is harsh in the world, whoredom rife—*
*an axe age, a sword age—shields are riven—*
*a wind age, a wolf age—before the world goes headlong.*
*No man will have mercy on another.*

VÖLUSPÁ, *THE POETIC EDDA*

"WANDERERS ARE BELOVED BY SHIVA," it is said in ancient texts. A traveler is thought to always be an image of Shiva. Perhaps reflecting this image, I was on the road again. Soft, thin clouds drifted slowly across the sunny, late-summer sky. Yogananda Puri and Savitri Puri, the Danish- and Swedish-born yogis I had befriended during my weeklong initiation in the countryside of Sweden and later at the Kumbh Mela in Hardwar, had taken me and my wife to a sacred site from the Viking Age, outside the city of Roskilde in Denmark (see color plate 12). Walking across a field to ancient stones with these two Scandinavian sadhus, initiates of an Indian esoteric doctrine, I wondered what was left to us of our own esoteric traditions that were perhaps whispered of at this site.

128

In ancient times, this had been a place for *blót,* sacrifice and worship. The large stones form ritualistic pathways and shapes that resemble ships surrounded by large mounds. To many modern people they would seem to be mere rocks, relics from a past of barbarism and heathen worship long gone and forgotten. But to a more discerning eye, their symbolism and significance is apparent.

The ship is more than a mere boat. It is the vessel in which passage across tumultuous waters takes place and as such is a traditional initiatory and magical symbol. In the ancient North, all journeys between worlds required a ship. Such journeys (which embodied a particular Nordic spirit of always *going beyond*) were passages from safe harbors to unknown shores or from the world of the living to the realm of the dead. Indeed, tribal chieftains would often be buried or burned along with their ships so they could be carried to the world beyond. The construction of such a great ship inevitably involved some form of magic or invocation of the gods.

Mirroring the sky, the ocean is the great unknown over which a voyage is undertaken. Its element, water, is forever shifting, borderless, and unfixed. Crossing the ocean can be likened to crossing the abyss. It is a frightful confrontation with not only death and temporality but also with the existential void and nihilism, which must be overcome by the sailor—the initiate-hero.

Seen in the light of such an understanding, what were mere stones and grave mounds in the past become something else. They are transformed into gateways and places of power where one can approach and connect with an impulse of the holy and the mysterious—that is, the meeting point of the time bound and the eternal. They echo a kind of understanding that would have been more readily apparent to our ancestors than it is to the people of our age. This is because, as many traditions attest, we live in an Age of Wolves.

Ours is an age of great dispossession. It is a time of war, terrorism, genocide, corruption, debasement, and economic and ecological disaster. But even more than these things, the great dispossession we face is an internal or spiritual one. This dispossession is discernable at almost every level of life and existence. Our gods, however we might perceive them, have left us. Our soul is barren and disconnected from the roots that nourished its growth and formation. We have lost our inner compass and are floundering around, aimless and lost, in pursuit of every joy and folly that this world has to offer and often coming up empty. We are adept at high technology and asserting dominion over nature, yet we do not master ourselves. We have knowledge, yet we lack wisdom. Rather than being allies, science and spirituality, the attempts by man to understand the nature of the world, are at odds with one another.

Most ancient teachings and cultures describe such end-times in their eschatologies. In the Indian tradition, this apocalyptic age is called the Kali Yuga. In the Germanic myth, it is called Ragnarök. In the Finnish epic poem *Kalevala,* a mythic device bringing happiness to its people, the Sampo, is shattered and lost in the sea. All of these mythic patterns clearly find their resonances in our time.

In the Indian tradition and its cyclical cosmology, there are four ages wherein the cosmos itself is created and destroyed, beginning with a golden age and ending in a final, iron age. This iron age is our age, the Kali Yuga. It is characterized by the loss of spiritual life and traditions and the valuing of everything through materialism and money. This final cycle is characterized by an escalation of degradation and conflict, culminating in the cataclysmic events that will end human life. Then Shiva, as destroyer and creator, dances his eternal dance, and time begins anew.

The ancient Puranas are remarkable in their detailed description of what characterizes this twilight time. They describe how society has deviated from nature and the natural law, turned its back on authentic spiritual tradition, and adopted arbitrary ideologies, moralistic and monotheistic religions, and pretentious, false prophets. How this degradation takes form in all realms of life is described in minute detail, from society, religion, culture, and language to sexuality and even food (i.e., "ready-made food will be sold").

The Puranas describe a process in which all values are inverted, a process of an accelerated "equalizing," a leveling in all spheres of existence, that is a prelude to the end. Observing the way things are around us, the Puranas seem to be accurate to an alarming degree—it is as if they are describing the world exactly as it now exists, poised on the brink of great cataclysmic events, all resulting from man himself.

Modern India is of course ripe with false prophets even wilder than those described in the Puranas. For example, a man who was the leader of a cult with tens of millions of followers and the writer, producer, choreographer, music composer, and star of his own blockbuster action movie convinced four hundred men to chop off their testicles as the only way to connect with god.

In the Nordic myth, the cataclysmic events that will bring an end to both gods and men is called Ragnarök, "twilight of the gods." It is the trickster god, Loki, who sets things in inevitable motion with his actions. Loki, god and/or *jötunn* (giant), possibly the blood brother of Odin, is the catalyst for change in the myths, causing the gods much consternation but equally often helping them out of dire situations as well. It is Loki who plots and causes the death of Balder, the sun god of light, beauty, joy, purity, justice, and harmony, heralding the end.

Ragnarök is preceded by Fimbulvinter, a time lasting three years during which summer does not come, and it snows constantly from all directions. During this "great winter," blood ties are no longer respected and war reigns.

The World Tree itself shudders and cries. In the final and fatal battle of Ragnarök, Loki and his children, the Midgård serpent Iormungandr and the Fenrir wolf, clash with the Aesir, the race of gods, including Odin, Thor, and Frey. The world is swallowed by fire before it is submerged in water (echoing a similar description in the Puranas). Out of this water, eventually a new green world shall emerge, repopulated by two humans, Líf and Lífþrasir (Life and Life-lust). And Balder, fairest of gods, will be reborn.

Central to the Finnish myth is the Sampo, a magical artifact forged by Ilmarinen, the sky forger, eternal hammerer, and blacksmith. This object brings might, health, and prosperity to its holders. When it gets stolen by the great witch of the North, Louhi, the homeland of Ilmarinen falls on hard times. In the battle for its retrieval, the Sampo falls and shatters and is lost in the sea. This item, whose precise nature is never revealed, seems to be a device or mill of some kind that creates abundance from thin air and has often been compared to the Holy Grail and the Greek cornucopia. According to a dominant theory, the Sampo is the World Tree or World Pillar itself, the central structure around which the universe, life, and time itself are ordered. And just as in the Germanic myth, in the end the World Tree is broken and submerged in the sea. Viewed in such a light, the Sampo seems less a physical object and more an intangible knowledge or wisdom, akin to the philosopher's stone of the alchemists, the loss of which caused great strife and misery for its people.

All of these things sprang into my mind when we walked around the desolate mounds in Denmark. And the Kali Yuga loomed ever present, as we wandered through other empty sacred sites across Europe. Once they were places of power, brimming with life. Now they were like graves of the old gods.

Back in the town where they lived, I watched Savitri remove her shoes, kneel, and perform her oblations by the holy spring of Saint John, Sankt Hans Kilde. It is one of many of such springs revered since ancient times for its pure water with reputedly healing qualities. According to legend, the waters were especially potent around the festival of midsummer. The sick were brought here to drink from special ceramic cups, which were smashed to pieces right after being used (wise, considering

Fig. 8.1. The author with Savitri Puri and
Yogananda Puri at Lejre, Denmark
(Photograph by Justine Cederberg)

it prevented diseases from spreading, even before people had knowledge about contagions). These days, a sign by the fountain says, ironically, "Water not for human consumption."

During the age of Kali Yuga, water is scarce, polluted, and must be bought. The fountains of the past, revered in ancient times, have run dry. Those fountains flowed not just with water but with memory and wisdom.

Savitri recited her mantras and sprinkled water over her head. I knelt by the fountain and did the same in silence. The water felt cold and pure, as drops glistened in the sunlight. The air was still and calm, and there were no people in sight. In the distance, church bells rang.

For several days we stayed in a guest room in the basement of Yogananda's and Savitri's house, which functioned as a yoga school. The basement also held their mandir. Early each morning, I could hear the ringing of bells followed by a litany of mantras, as Yogananda entered to perform his morning rites. A faint scent of incense lingered through the hallway.

In an old sauna in the hippie commune of Freetown Christiania, I watched Yogananda; having removed his *lingoti* (loincloth of the Naga Babas) and smeared his skin with dark gray clay, he was sitting naked and cross-legged on the floor of the shower room. His eyes were half-closed in meditation, while the sun shone through the window on his stonelike body. He reminded me of a statue of Shiva then—more than a human being; present in this world, but at the same time, somehow above and detached from it as well.

Later, as we were walking, immersed in deep dialogue, I was trying to see the line where our worlds converged and parted. Our discussion was interrupted by a young man: "Spare money for drugs?" Yogananda took out his little bag and gave him some cash. "It is Friday the thirteenth, after all," he said smilingly.

Our dialogues continued at night in the temple, lined with murtis, familiar from years back when they were present at my initiation. It was during our long nightly dialogues that I realized how much shadow there really was surrounding all the supposed "love and light" of the Indian esoteric world.

The Puranas emphasize how false gods, ideals, and prophets, along with degraded holy men, are a sign of the times:

"Even the teachings are sold."

"Priests will degrade themselves by selling the sacraments."

"Hermits (*vanaprastha*) will eat the food of the middle class, and monks (sannyasis) will have amorous relationships (*sneha-sambandha*) with their friends."

"Adventurers will take on the appearance of monks, with shaven heads, orange clothing, and rosary beads around their necks."

"People will accept theories promulgated by anyone as articles of faith. False gods will be worshipped in false ashrams in which fasts, pilgrimages, penances, donation of possessions, and austerities in the name of the would-be religion will be arbitrarily decreed. People of low birth will put on religious costumes and, by their behavior, will make themselves respected."*

In light of these passages, it perhaps is no surprise that even the sadhus and yogis, who are ostensibly the keepers and upholders of timeless traditions, are far from immune to the age of Kali Yuga.

I had witnessed Yogananda's and Savitri's initiations into Naga Babas during the Kumbh Mela in Hardwar. Now, some years later, much had changed. Surely it was incredibly difficult, if not altogether impossible, for Europeans such as them to live as Naga Babas in the modern Western world. But even more than that, Yogananda and Savitri had fallen out with their guru, Rampuri. Without going into details of their rift, which are and should remain their private matter, it was with sadness that I recognized a certain look on my friends' faces,

---

*All of these quotations from the Puranas have been taken from Daniélou, *While the Gods Play,* 212–13.

that stinging, bitter pain of disillusionment. Their teacher had been at the epicenter of their lives. Now, instead, there was hollowness.

Yogananda dealt with this rift through discipline, as he seemed to do with all things. Just as I had seen him sitting in meditation like Shiva Shankara on a mountaintop, unmoved by the world below, I could see him similarly detached from recent upheavals.

For Savitri, it had been more difficult. I was told about her episode of "divine madness," which had happened during Navratri, and incidentally, also on the date of their break with Rampuri. As the events unfolded, Savitri had fallen into a kind of altered or possessed state. Not sleeping, she had consumed alcohol and cooked omelets, although she had been a longtime abstainer from alcohol and a vegetarian. Savitri had erected little altars throughout the house, made almost constant pujas, disappeared into the forest at night, and climbed a tree. These events had created an unnerving and negative atmosphere in the house, which their students and guests had sensed.

In the Western world, behaviors such as these are viewed strictly as pathologies and mental illnesses. Through the lens of modern medical science, nothing good can ever come from such aberrations—they are mere delusions. However, in other, less rationally oriented societies still infused with magical traditions, such episodes are often seen in a more shamanic light. In the ancient world, extraordinary experiences were thought of as an ability to be in contact with other realms of reality beyond the apparent—perhaps even something that could bring prosperity to the community. Where does the border lie between mental illness and shamanic states of ecstasy?

Obviously these are gray, culture-bound areas, but one thing is clear: in a society lacking any mythical or magical context for "irrational" states, the confines of sanity are incredibly shallow. Savitri was perhaps burdened with a special sensitivity for such states. She looked vulnerable and said in a hushed voice, as if submitting to her destiny, "I know it will happen again."

I was reminded of Goethe's poem about the sorcerer's apprentice who calls forth powerful spirits he cannot control. Yogananda blamed it all on a dark, malevolent "trickster spirit," which he thought had possessed Savitri. The murky territory of spirits, the malevolent and benevolent personalities of nature, was often brought up casually in conversations with yogis and given credit for extraordinary events, whereas in my view, the events probably had entirely human origins. I could see how unnecessarily giving credence to spirits instead of looking for human agents led to denial of responsibility. At the same time, there are forces that affect us that we cannot govern or understand, and it is arrogant to think we do. It is therefore wise to shield oneself from malevolent influences and be careful about just what or whom one chooses to invoke.

Upon hearing about Savitri "climbing a tree" during the festival of Nine Nights, I immediately thought of the story of Odin's initiation. For nine nights Odin hung wounded from the World Tree—the tree that "no one knows from which root it rises." In great pain and hunger he hung there, a sacrifice of "himself to himself." Finally, howling, Odin took the runes, "the secrets," and fell down from the tree.

This story seemed to have a strange resemblance to aspects of Savitri's experience. Odin, after all, was like Shiva: the wild shamanic god of consciousness, wisdom, and death, who, in order to gain secret knowledge, had sacrificed one eye to Mimir's well (the well of memory) and hence had one eye always in this world and one in the other. I told this story to my friends, as I thought that perhaps Savitri as a Swede could relate to these Odinic myths and find some solace from them. Perhaps connecting with the divinities of her own homeland might ground her in a way that invoking foreign gods could not.

One thing I had certainly learned during my delving into the esoteric world of India was how things were *not*. The guru is at least ideally the "dispeller of darkness," and I certainly had many illusions shattered—which was all for the better. I had started to look at things differently, to measure things according to different standards, to seek authenticity.

The so-called spirituality of the West today is, rather than an antidote for the Kali Yuga, a symptom of it. The dominant Western religions in their current form are void of vitality and élan—they can no longer sustain and nurture the spirit, if they indeed ever did. The same goes for most of what falls in the realm of so-called alternative spirituality. It is almost always incredibly superficial and hopelessly imbalanced, erring too much on one side or the other: either the nauseating, neurotic "lightness" of the New Age or its opposite, the childish affection toward all things dark and morbid.

Lacking authority, much of what passes as "esoteric tradition" in the West is resting on little more than the flimsy ideas and idle speculation of its makers. Often shunning its own inherent pagan traditions, lore, and wisdom, the West freely borrows and adopts foreign traditions from supposedly "more spiritual" (often more primitive) cultures and, ultimately, misappropriates them. The sedate, feminine, and commercial world of modern Western yoga, for instance, seems like the exact inverted mirror image of traditional yoga as I had come to see it in India. How different are the Naga Babas, those wild, untamed god-crazed yogis of old, from the starry-eyed health-and-fitness enthusiasts veiled in Indian aesthetics that we have grown accustomed to in the West.

The motive, of course, for many modern movements is often all too familiar: monetary gain (and sometimes sexual favors). But then again, echoing even the sentiments of some traditional gurus in India, magic has seemingly always been done for power and sex.

I had also come to realize that beyond the complicated organizational structures of the akharas, the Naga Babas are a spiritual gang. They form a hierarchical, dominantly male world, a brotherhood. They are a family, fiercely loyal to each other and to their internal order. They are organized as warriors, having a long history of militancy, fighting rival groups and Muslims in the past, and later, the British.

Great power lies in such alliances. In India, the Naga Babas are a real force and authority to be reckoned with. In previous Kumbh Melas, disputes about the order of bathing had led to violent riots with casualties, as Naga Sadhus had used their trishuls as weapons. I remember a high-ranking policeman working in the anti-terrorism forces at the Kumbh Mela, humbly sitting along with everyone else by a Naga Baba dhuni, being a devotee. It was also not uncommon to see Naga Babas shouting at soldiers, who would obey them without question.

The Naga Babas moved at the periphery of society and were fierce, joyful, independent, loyal more to themselves than to a state, and, if necessity dictated, violent. There was nothing inherently wrong with any of this.

However, at the Kumbh Mela in Hardwar, I had seen a line that was not to be crossed. I deeply appreciated being a guest and friend at the Juna Akhara camp. I gained a glimpse into the world of the Naga Babas and the authentic Indian esoteric tradition that is not available to many Westerners. My initiation was and would remain a talisman for me, and my name in that world would always be the one I was given—Adinath Puri. I respected the Naga Babas and their world, although I could not understand some of the more extreme aspects of it (such as the severe self-mortification). I had learned much from my interaction with that world—but it was not *my* world, *my* brotherhood. I did not share common spiritual roots, ancestry, and language with the Naga Babas, and hence, would always remain an outsider in their midst. And that was as it should be. There were tribal connections to be sought in the lands of my own *jâti* (clan), slumbering ancestral gods waiting to be reawakened.

I no longer felt the need for a mentor. Guided by my inner visions, I had come far enough where I was not dependent on outside validation for my path. The mentors I had encountered, old masters who were partially real individuals and partially images I had created for myself, would always be there as streams running through my life—but they were not its fountain.

In the Norse myth, the god of light and beauty, Balder, is slain and dwells in the underworld, Hel, to be reborn after Ragnarök and herald a new green earth. The Finnish epic *Kalevala* in turn ends with the old god of poetry and magic, Väinämöinen, leaving his kantele and song for the children of his land, rowing away from the lands of men to distant shores, perhaps one day to return to "forge a new Sampo" for his people. According to the Puranas: "The end of the Kali Yuga is a particularly favorable period to pursue knowledge. . . . The god Shiva will appear to reestablish the right path in a secret and hidden form."

In a time when most are debased, there will remain men who will keep to their true nature and rediscover the teachings enshrined in esoteric traditions, such as Shaivism, gnosticism, and various ancestral pagan religions. These men will be a refuge in whom timeless values and wisdom can be embodied, and in them will lie the seeds of a new world beyond the collapse of the current one. By necessity, these men will stand apart from the modern world. In an age when timeless, archaic, natural truths are rejected because they rarely align with modern, more progressive ideas, these men will perhaps find little solace in the civilized world as it is. They will be shunned, destined to live as barbarians, outsiders, outcasts, wandering at the periphery of society, at the borderland between civilization and primal nature, which are often at odds with one another. In our age of iron, they will have to become wolves themselves.

On our last night at Yogananda and Savitri's house, we rang the bells while entering their temple for a traditional evening puja. We sat down and shared some of Shiva's resin. Before smoking I lifted the chillum up to my forehead, and shouted "Bom!" Inhaling deeply through my fingers, as is custom, I felt the smoke fill my lungs before drifting out into the air in front of me as a thick, blue-gray mist, the color of which reminded me of the skin of Shiva. Yoganada and Savitri looked on and smiled.

The temple was lit by candles and ghee lights, and my eyes wandered from statue to statue, gazing at those serene faces overlooking us. I felt the presence of Bholenath, the lord of intoxicating substances, as Yogananda conducted the rite. Savitri started singing a Shiva mantra and, after listening to her, I joined in. The melody was familiar from somewhere in the past, and yet calmer, more beautiful and somehow more melancholic as well.

Serenity quickly faded as bells, drums, and horns resounded in the air to get the attention of the gods, a divine cacophony that reverberated through the house and shook the windows. Aartis to Ganesh, Shiva, and Dattatreya followed—most of which I had learned to sing in India years ago. Smoke, sound, and song filled the room, as the statues of the gods came alive and cast flickering shadows on the walls. We each lay a flower at an image; I lay mine at the feet of Saraswati, the goddess of wisdom and language. The dry taste of vibhuti, sacred ash, mixed familiarly in my mouth with the sweet prasad of apples, dates, and peanuts.

Afterward, we sat in the temple late into the night, talking and smoking more chillums. The ghee lights flickered and went out slowly, one by one. As we exited the temple, I touched both of my yogi friends' feet.

The following morning, before leaving, we stretched out in a large white room flooded with sunlight. I shadowboxed a few rounds, and watched the play of light and dark of my figure on the wooden floor. My shadow felt intimate to me, like an old friend.

We drove through Copenhagen to the old Carlsberg beer brewery, the outer walls of which were flanked by figures of Hermes, messenger of the gods and mediator between the human and the divine, as well as Fortuna, goddess of fortune, luck, and fate. Giant Indian-style stone elephants guarded the gates with massive swastikas on their sides.

I raised my eyes to the highest rooftop and saw a triumphant statue of Thor, holding his hammer aloft while riding his goat-pulled chariot over giants (see color plate 13). What would the world look like now had we, the people of the North, not abandoned our gods in favor of some foreign creed? In that eternal moment, as I gazed at the thunder god's dominant figure gleaming in the sunlight, something everlasting echoed through the ages. Perhaps the old gods are not gone after all, although their statues are few and their names seldom spoken. Perhaps they will yet again reveal themselves to us in our time of need, in new forms.

The late summer sky was blue, and I could feel the strong familiar breeze of a northern wind.

# 9
# DREAMS OF FORGOTTEN GODS

*To be a poet in a destitute time means: to attend, singing,*
*to the trace of the fugitive gods.*
*This is why the poet in the time of the world's night utters*
*the holy.*

MARTIN HEIDEGGER

AFTER MANY JOURNEYS FAR AND WIDE, the circle comes to a close. I find myself alone in the old ancestral house of my family, in the forest by the sea. All of my dreams and travels had finally led me home, back to this place where my restless spirit can find some respite.

It is late November as I write these words. During this cruelest of months in the north, it becomes dark after three o'clock in the afternoon. The sun does not shine for weeks on end, and days are mere fleeting hours of vague twilight that soon give way to starless nights. Skeletal trees shiver against an infinitely gray sky, the sea roars and rages, and the wind howls, seemingly indifferent to living creatures, who are nowhere to be seen. The forests and fields lose their colors and become permeated by an insurmountable barrenness. At this time of year, my senses yearn for the saving grace of winter, when all comes to a standstill and all that was impure and decaying is hidden under a fresh layer of snow, transforming even the ugliest of things into statues—the poetry of nature, then, becomes less cruel and more gentle, more merciful. But for now, I have to keep the lights on and the fires burning.

In front of me opens the wide ocean. It stretches to the horizon and beyond, almost merging with the uniform gray sky, where a faint pink tear of light breaks, as if someone cut through a theater backdrop with a knife. Behind me are the woods of my childhood, in which evergreens hover and hum in a deep, earthly tone. On the forest hill close by, there are still traces of moss-swallowed paths that I built from stone as a boy. They lead to a large fallen trunk, under the branches of which I had a hideout, and then disappear suddenly. This arboreal landscape is like my soul—deep and dark, sometimes almost impenetrable, full of hidden paths that dissolve, and, yet, also paths that lead to sudden clearings in the woods where all paths converge.

Between the sea and the forest stands my old ancestral house. In the central room, the darkened timber walls are lined with age-old family tapestries woven by my grandparents and ancestral portraits, whose faces remind me of my own. In this room, past lives and my childhood sense of wonder come alive once again. Experiencing the awe evoked by a thunderstorm rattling the old windows and watching the sky being torn up by lightning, I instinctually realized what was meant by a god of thunder. In the tales and stories I heard at my grandmother's feet by the warmth of the crackling fireplace, I glimpsed something of the nature of the greater narrative, how she was telling stories of fates not so different from my own.

One morning on the veranda, I watched my grandfather, sitting in his rocking chair, smoking a pipe, suddenly clasp his chest, keel over, and die. For the first time, I was given permission to gather flowers from the garden behind the house, which I then carefully laid out on my grandfather's chest. His body had been carried into the middle of the central room I am sitting in now and where I sleep during these cold November nights.

Also on the walls of this room are large runes, which had hung from the branches of the tree under which my wife and I were married. In my mind's eye, I still see them swinging in the wind—the runes for protection, joy, gift, and homeland—which now guard each cardinal point of the room.

In my dreams I always return here. Like some sort of mythic Ur home, this place has a magnetic pull that draws me to it. And so I sit by the fireplace, surrounded by ancestors, memories, dreams, and darkness. I hear only the waves of the sea and the crackling fire and, sometimes, when it is quiet enough, the hovering, creaking pines. My mind wanders along the moss-devoured stone paths that I had built as a child, and I think about where the paths I have traveled have led me. In a sense, I have returned to the place of my grandmother's stories—the heroic, mythic world, whose motifs still play a prominent part in the unfolding story of my life. Here, by the hearth of my ancestral house, surrounded by silence and shadows, I am at the crossing of all things.

To retain their meaning, pilgrimages have to come to an end. Ultimately, one *must* return home, lest one become a wanderer in the winds, blown here and there, forever on the move. When I entered the world of journeying, I was a mere youthful pilgrim, an explorer fueled by a thirst for experience, knowledge, and finally, wisdom. In the course of time, I have grown from that youthful pilgrim to a man nearing the midway of his life. Now my mind is occupied by thoughts of roots, of family, of home, and, for once, of stopping my wanderings and letting things grow.

But still, there is much of the youthful explorer in me. As the only visible lights on a dark ocean are the distant lamps of the ships far out at sea, an old wanderlust overtakes me—a restlessness perhaps never satiated. I hear the waves, and they speak the language of the sailor's blood

Fig. 9.1. The Odal rune, pictured here above the author's ancestral hearth, points toward sacred enclosure, tribal inheritance, heritage, and homeland. (Photograph by Constantine Morte)

coursing in my veins. I am not comfortable with mere contemplation yet; there is still much action in me. But maybe I have ceased longing to find some *thing* and instead sought a way *to be,* an inner experience mirroring that of our highest aspirations—those that some call gods, others call cosmic being, and still others call destiny. Those highest aspirations can most readily be accessed in harmony with one's own nature and through a connection with the soil from which one springs, where roots have grown for several lifetimes. They form a magical link to the mythic landscapes and spiritual world of our ancestors, which are our sacred inheritance.

At the same, to know the highest aspirations, one has to be intimate with the lowest, darkest crevasses as well. Those lowest impulses seem to take hold whenever man loses his innate balance and forgets from whence he sprung; when he becomes disconnected from nature both without and within, and when universalist messiahs and demagogues raid the seats where his tribal gods sat before. Man is always poised at the intersection of the greatest peaks and the deepest valleys, standing perpetually at a precipice that seems to be carved into his very being. At no time has this been more apparent than right now. The month of November reflects our own time in many ways. It is an in-between time, a barren time, a time of decay. It is a time of slumbering and dark stillness. Yet outside, somewhere, the world seems to be burning. Only a few days ago a large-scale terrorist attack happened in my beloved city of Paris. It was not the first nor the last terrorist attack in the world or in the West, and not even the one I was closest to when it happened (there were several close calls when I was in India, each time perpetrated by the same people acting under the same god and prophet). But somehow this incident moved and disturbed me profoundly. A dystopia seemed to be unfolding itself in front of my eyes. Discontent and disarray were growing, and I felt powerless in the face of these events. The constant bad news, distraction, and polarizing chatter of the media was disheartening, and I needed distance to see it all clearly. I longed to return to some source and serenity outside of these apocalyptic currents, so as to not get swept under along with them. As I left the city, the headlines of the major evening newspapers screamed, EUROPE IS AT WAR!

Struggles are fought, won, and lost, as they have been for centuries, but the wars rage on. Often these wars are conducted seemingly under the rule of demonic, tyrannical desert gods or barren demagogues that want to divide and conquer and impose their chains across all of humanity. Lives are given and taken, as human sacrifices for these gods and their followers. I had never given much credence to the gnostic idea of a Demiurge, a false ruler and creator of this imperfect world, a cruel, ignorant, and tyrannical entity at the heart of earthly suffering and stupidity, restricting human beings' entry into higher levels of existence—but in light of recent events, this had started to make much more sense to me.

Although man has to stand and take responsibility for his own actions, at times I was forced to wonder if there in fact was something that man had fallen sway to. It seemed as if there was a long-standing war waging between higher and lower forces of consciousness, between the debased and the elevated, for the chasm between these two seemed to be ever widening.

At night, I contemplated the fire. During the day, I watched the heavy gray clouds block out the half-light for the few meager hours the sun was above the horizon. In the evening, I stood naked at the stormy seashore, facing the waves, in defiance of the wind, cold, and darkness. In such times, there is only inner illumination to guide one's way—only the inner flame. As I searched my spirit for this flame, I came to see strands that grew ever more apparent.

Whirlwinds of numinous experience washed over me, bathing me in knowledge that would perhaps, over time, be churned into wisdom. Upon returning from far voyages, one has to take stock of what one has found, even if what was sought was something intangible. What had I learned? What was the nature of the gods and the sacred that I was seeking? What gifts did I bring back from other worlds?

At times I felt as if it was perhaps all illusory, that I had not truly found anything at all except for my own thirst to create some meaning in a meaningless world. And then, at other moments, struck by the awe of some suddenly flowering part of my soul, I again saw the strands of my life shining brighter than before, and they were not random. Those strands were a constant searching, a waging of a spiritual war in the face of nothingness, a sometimes bitter battle against all odds and reason and rationality—yet they were sincere, pure, even noble strands, reaching for a hidden, forgotten truth.

My life had been a long journey during which I sought to give form to inner landmarks and symbols that I encountered in dreams and visions and find their equivalents in the waking world. It was a soaring seeking of the divine in its highest possible form conceivable to me as a human being. These strands showed me the lifeline of my existence, which had been dedicated to this quest. I turned, then, to those moments where this lifeline had coursed the most violently, the most fully, and I came upon traces of fleeting gods.

And so, it ends as it began.

Two decades ago I had a dream that dramatically altered the course of my life. It came to me in a time of personal crisis. I had arrived at dead ends on many paths and was plagued by a soul sickness, an all-devouring dispossession. It seemed that all solutions had exhausted themselves for me, that I had lost my way and was on the losing side of a hopeless battle. Then, in the midst of this dark night of the soul, a dream appeared to me.

I dreamt of a forgotten god.

In the dream, I was walking through a market that sold religious and spiritual icons, statues, and relics. The stalls were lined with deities, demons, saints, creatures, and mythic figures from various cultures, traditions, and pantheons. I continued walking through the market and past the stalls, until I came to a simple wooden table. On the table was a small bronze statuette of a god sitting cross-legged. He was bearded, wore a pointed cap, and was perhaps drinking something out of a horn. He also had an engorged phallus. I took the statue in my hand, and as I did so, a great sense of clarity and renewed purpose came over me. I did not then recognize the god that the statue represented but realized that I had found something of great significance.

Upon awakening, I was profoundly moved by the majesty of the dream. Who was this god whose image I had so readily wandered over to and taken as my own? Where do such images emerge from? If one finds something valuable in a dream, does it vanish when one awakens or can one retain part of it?

I had encountered an ancestral god. It was a god who was somehow kin to me, standing above and behind me like an unknown forefather, guiding me toward a common destiny, speaking to me through his image, from the liminal realms at the margins of consciousness.

I had perhaps seen the dream statuette somewhere before, but it took me a few minutes to consciously identify the figure that it depicted—and then I remembered: this cross-legged, ithyphallic deity was depicting the Nordic god Frey. Frey, whose name means "lord," is a deity from the northern heathen tradition associated with sacred kingship and ancestry. He is thought of as a powerful guardian of the sacred and a divine ancestor, hence one of his names is *blótgoda* (sacrifice priest). His blessings include those of *ár*—"prosperity and abundance," especially as they relate to the land—and *friðr* (sacred inviolability).* Frey, whose festivals are those of midsummer and midwinter, is also associated with oath taking, virility, fertility, sea journeys, and weather. According to the Icelandic sagas, the Eddas, Frey stems from an older family of gods, the Vanir, who preceded the Aesir into which he was later adopted. Thus, he is part of two divine races: one associated with earth and the other with sky. His father is the sea god Njörðr. Frey is also the twin brother and occasional

---

*Ann Gróa Sheffiled, *Frey: God of the World* (Lulu.com, 2002).

lover of Freya, the goddess of war, *seiðr* sorcery, and love and sexuality, who is responsible for teaching Odin himself the secrets of magic.

Frey is commonly thought of as one of the central triad of male deities of the northern pantheon, along with Odin and Thor. His cult was stronger in Sweden than anywhere else in Scandinavia, and numerous groves, fields, and forests are named after him. Old Uppsala in southern Sweden was central to the Frey cult, as the temple there was said to have been built by the god himself. Adam of Bremen, the eleventh-century Christian writer, described it thusly:

> In this temple, entirely decked out in gold, the people worship the statues of three gods . . . in such wise that the mightiest of them, Thor, occupies a throne in the middle of the chamber; Wotan [Odin] and Frikko [Frey] have places on either side. The significance of these gods is as follows: Thor, they say, presides over the air, which governs the thunder and lightning, the winds and rains, fair weather and crops. The other, Wotan—that is, the Furious—carries on war and imparts to man strength against his enemies. The third is Frikko, who bestows peace and pleasure on mortals. His likeness, too, they fashion with an immense phallus.*

Sometimes called Yngvi-Freyr and Ingunar Frey, he is also thought of as the ancestor of the Ynglingarna royal dynasty of Swedish kings. Indeed, Frey is connected to sacred kingship to such an extent that the stories of kings are often assimilated with stories of the god, as both have a similar role in governing a good year of prosperity and peace. Both god and king are guardians of the sacred, maintainers of divine order. Later, Frey himself was said to have been buried in one of the mounds at Uppsala; hence he is perceived as the "god of the grave mound," who receives sacrifices and in return, grants blessings.

---

*Adam of Bremen, *Gesta Hammaburgensis ecclesiae pontificum* [Deeds of the Bishops of Hamburg], 1043–1072.

One of the central stories of Frey involves him becoming lovesick over the beautiful giantess Gerda, whom he has a vision of while sitting on Odin's high seat. To marry the object of his love, Frey gives up his magical sword, which fights as by itself "if wise the hands that wield it." As a consequence, he fights in the great battle of Ragnarök, the twilight of the gods, armed only with an antler.

Be all that as it may, before my dream, Frey was a figure that I had only peripheral knowledge of—if even that. I certainly had not chosen the figure that I found in my dream in any conscious manner, nor had he ever seemed relevant to me. But from somewhere this ancient god had now arisen and his presence was strong. That morning and during the days following, I delved into the myths of Frey. Myths are images of our earliest memories, ageless wisdom, and sacred reality, which is beyond the temporal and the profane, and they have been said to be things that "never happened, but always are."*

The more I read about Frey, the more I found I was reading about *myself;* the more I learned, the more the mythic merged with the leitmotif of my own life. I saw my dream as being touched by "the shining one" (one of Frey's titles). In such dreams, the veils between worlds are thin, and the spirit harkens back to its home in eternity. The lovesickness of Frey represents, then, not a longing for a person or a being but of a homesickness for wholeness and holiness, a longing for the state that is the soul's true homeland.

There are decisive moments in life during which one has to make a choice whether to trust signs and visions as they emerge, to make talismans out of dreams and follow them—convenient or not—or to discard them as curious but ultimately hollow fantasies of the psyche. For me, there was hardly a choice. Although I was never without doubts about whether I was chasing after mere desert mirages, I trusted the rare visions I had and sought their form in the causal world. Perhaps

---

*Sallustius, *Concerning the Gods and the Universe,* fourth century CE.

it is the gods, whatever they are, that whisper to us at these times. For as long as I could remember, I had felt connected to ancient hidden divinities, starkly different from the ones being propagated by the major monotheistic world religions. These gods were hidden because mankind seemed to have forgotten them. Yet their presence lingered, peering from the edge of memory and knowledge, ready to burst forth in times of need or upheaval, when facades crumbled and something more primal emerged from under the surface.

Such were the gods of ancient India and Europe, who in times past seemed to share common ground. Shiva, for instance, resembled the god Dionysus, and their cults were strikingly similar. "Dionysos is not a man: he is an animal and at the same time, a god, thus manifesting the extremes of the opposing characteristics in man himself."* The nature of these gods was not dogmatic and confined to boundaries of rationality and creed; it was ecstatic and could be experienced directly and personally. Likewise, so it was with the gods of the Northlands.

As nature desires to know itself, so it is our fate that we try to fathom the unknowable, to reach for that which is beyond our grasp. Time and again, I find myself returning to the Nordic myths, where this never-ending search is so vividly expressed. In Finnish myth, the rune-singer god Väinämöinen travels into the underworld to gain secret words. For the same purpose Odin, the Nordic god of magic, hung on the World Tree for nine nights, "on that tree of which no man knows from where its roots run."

Both northern myths mirror the shamans and *tietäjä* (knowers) of old who would, like the gods, fall into trance and enter other worlds to gain secrets (i.e., knowledge) to bring back to the tribe. In battle, gods of thunder and frenzy would be invoked and embodied by warrior bands; in love, gods of ecstasy and prosperity would take seat in the flesh of lovers. Emulating and embodying the gods and goddesses, one

---

*Giorgio Colli, quote from *La sapienza greca* in Daniélou, *Gods of Love and Ecstasy,* 112.

could begin to know them. Contemplating signs and runes, one could become aligned with the mind of the divine.

I had witnessed the same divine emulation firsthand in India among the Shaivite Babas, who took on the characteristics, attributes, emblems, and even outer appearance of their lord in order to know him, to embody him, to *become* him. Sadly in Europe and the modern Western world, recognition of such figures has been largely lost. What lies beyond the rational, unable to be readily grasped, defined, categorized, and dissected must lie in the realm of pathology. Our minds have become dull in the face of what is strange, beautiful, terrifying, and mysterious—in a word, godlike. And yet, beyond ideas, abstractions, and all that comes from mere intellect lies the immediate, numinous phenomena itself, which still retains its wild, earth-shattering potentiality.

The ancient god and divine ancestor of my dream appeared to me not as a deity to worship but as guide who illuminated a path. To receive him as a protector meant to take on his characteristics, to become like him. He was the guardian of the holy, and the holy was what needed presencing.

After months of dreary haziness, it was my dream that made me set out on a long journey over the sea, as did Frey in the myths. So it was that I left my home within days of my vision. It was this journey that set me on a path I am still traversing today. It was also this journey, under the patronage of an ancestral god, that ultimately cured me of my soul sickness. I gained back my will to fight and partake once more in the drama of human life, which is reflected time and again in the mythic narratives. In the great final twilight battle of Ragnarök, the gods set out against giant enemies knowing that they will die. And yet they face their fate with joy and defiance.

This might also be the path that we have to embark on as Europeans, as people that share a spiritual and cultural heritage, both inner and outer landscapes, and a common destiny if we wish to cure ourselves of the ills that plague us. For surely, beyond the current and inevitable struggles and their dire results of wide-scale human suffering, Europe is engaged in a spiritual war. It is a war fought not only against an outer enemy but also an inner one. It is a war against a self-defeating nothingness, against an all-consuming loss of spirit, against a desacralization of the world and nature now at sway across our lands. Political solutions to this war can offer only a temporary respite, as time-bound problems are symptoms of a deeper malaise, and the war will go on until such issues are dealt with.

Nature and the world have been stripped of their majesty and mystery—all that remains for us is gross matter and its exploitation. Our inner world, equally, has been laid bare. Materialism, nihilism, and a kind of sad hedonism abound, resulting in a weary resignation of defeat. The things that were to set us free have ended up enslaving us. The screens of computers and smartphones illuminate our faces in the dark, as once did the fires around which we sat. We have created a world in which we have become strangers. At the global marketplace of religions and ideologies, we are offered a selection of universalist creeds—whether monotheistic religions or their various ideological counterparts—that reduce man to a mere economic unit.

All of these things only disconnect us further from our tribal nature, from the all-encompassing force of the divine. Our so-called leaders, both religious and political, care more for abstract, globalist concepts than for their own people. In India the Hindu temples, festivals, and holy places are guarded by legions of armed soldiers, while our holiest of holies lie wide open, unprotected; often we have forgotten that they even exist. It is a collective dark night of the soul.

And yet people cannot live forever in a state of decline, discontent, and disconnection from their true being. What is needed is not another arbitrary ideology, but a rekindling of holy fires, a reconnection with the wisdom of the sacred soil and soul we are a part of. Perhaps we need to reach for our roots and dream strongly of our tribal gods, harkening back to the deep daimonic wells of memory and knowledge. Pyres should be lit and oneiric vigils made in honor of those old gods who lie dormant that they might awaken and appear again. For European man is an arboreal creature: just like a tree, he cannot live without his deepest roots or his highest branches reaching toward the sun. That sun is the hidden heart and soul of Europe.

The more I traveled in faraway lands, the more I felt connected to my own inherited spiritual landscapes. It had become apparent that for most of the Western individuals I knew their initiation into the Indian esoteric world had not been entirely successful or without considerable trials. Although the divine takes on infinite manifestations and forms, there is seldom a good reason for a European person to worship Hindu deities, which are, in essence, the folkish deities of particular Indian peoples that rose from the local relationships of those people with the holy, specific to them and their lands. For instance, there is something strange in revering Saraswati in Europe, for Europe has its own river goddesses. Some people even sadly err so far in their search for some dark and macabre power that they invoke forces that might even be harmful and hostile to them.

All of this is not to say that a great deal cannot be learned and experienced from different traditional cultures or that the divine cannot be approached through them, because it certainly can. One should view various foreign traditions of wisdom with the respect they merit, ideally, though perhaps not likely, leading to a form of mutually respectful religious plurality. Yet in the soil one naturally springs from there is an immediacy and an intimacy that would be foolish to overlook. A wholesale adoption of foreign deities and ways of spiritual practice is, barring some exceptions, often confusing and even counterproductive for it does not bring one closer to yoga—that is, "union."

This brings to mind a story told to me by Rampuri. When he visited one of the Baltic countries to give satsang and perform aarti, the hosts were worried that there was not enough gangajal (holy water from the river Ganga) for the ceremony. Rampuri reminded them that they had just passed a river with an auspicious name that had been considered holy since ancient times and suggested that they collect some of that indigenous water instead. Holiness is not just something found in India; the holy is everywhere and permeates everything. Likewise, a spiritual tradition is not something one can pick and choose; it is something already inside oneself, a whole world that need only be nurtured to grow.

I contemplated what I had learned from my interaction with the Indian esoteric tradition and how this knowledge could be applied to the West, which has largely lost touch with its own wisdom traditions. During all of my travels in the ancient mythic realms of India and Nepal, there was one constant that had become ever more clear: I needed to search for those "crossing-over places" where the holy is manifested in my own hereditary landscapes and culture. This had been a natural impulse for me even before any of my far journeys, but confronted by an age-old civilization where the mythical and magical were still alive, where a form of monistic pagan polytheism was still practiced, it had grown to occupy a central position in my life.

The conclusions I arrived at were echoed in those of esoteric thinkers of the past, such as traditionalist author René Guénon: "It is thus only a question, in short, of reconstituting that which existed before the modern deviation, with those adaptions necessary for the conditions of a different era. . . . the East may well be able to come to the rescue of the West, if the latter really wants it, not in order to impose strange concepts, as some people seem to fear, but to help the West rediscover its own tradition whose meaning has been lost."*

Could archaic streams of knowledge and tradition and mythopoetic thinking and engaging with the world, be breathed with new life in a meaningful way? Could this kind of knowledge be combined with

---

*René Guénon, *The Crisis of the Modern World* (Hillsdale, N.Y.: Sophia Perennis, 2001), 36.

modern science and technology in a meeting of physics and metaphysics? Could the old gods and our sense of them return and guide our way to the future?

There can be no revival of past forms belonging to ages long gone. There can be no nostalgia for those aspects of the past that were crude, unsophisticated, and superstitious. Let us cast aside ancient taboos and now meaningless customs. Force and form are needed to present only the core essence of what has been lost. That essence can and should take a multitude of shapes.

It is also delusional to harbor false idealism for any large-scale spiritual movement or force of change arising from "the people." Seeds for something beyond our present state are always sown by the select few, by individuals who stand above the modern world and their time. These are the rare ones that have the vision to see beyond the current dreary landscapes, that have the language to give voice to the fiery stirrings of the deepest caverns and most dizzying heights of their soul.

On a quest to see these issues clearly, I made pilgrimages to the sacred sites of Europe. From hyperborean regions beyond the north wind to the regal mountains of the south, from eastern woodlands to western cliffs at the end of the earth, I searched for streams of tradition and knowledge that would reflect the rays of the secret sun.*

In my youth, I erroneously thought that I was following a silent, solitary religion. Yet the more I traveled, the more I realized that this religion was already a hidden reality, taking shape simultaneously in different cultures, in esoteric and exoteric forms, all radiating from the same source. Over the years, upon meeting people throughout the European homelands, I would find an instant kinship, a mutual spiritual understanding that was an affirmation of the underlying convergence of inner vistas I had already sensed within. Such encounters

---

*These travels, too many and varied to properly discuss here, will be the subject of a another book.

happened by sacred fires, under holy trees, by standing stones, on mountaintops, and in cavernous terrains, in temples, gardens, groves, and forests, by rivers and the sea, in cities, on quiet small-town lanes, and in countryside taverns. Often these chance meetings would within moments manifest as some extraordinary event, a magical coincidence, a ritual, a journey. Talismans were exchanged and libations were shared with new acquaintances as if they were old friends, connected by something intangible but very real.

Likewise, various movements were arising, giving voice to similar sentiments. People were responding to the spiritual alienation of the modern world by seeking a return to more rooted ways of being. In Iceland, the native religion of Ásatrú based on the Nordic gods, represented by the Ásatrúarfélagið (Ásatrú Fellowship, which was recognized as a registered religious organization in 1973), is building its first *hof,* or temple, in over a thousand years. Its architecture is based on sacred geometry (specifically, the number nine), and it will house seasonal celebrations as well as weddings and funerals.

In the Baltics, the modern continuation of the ancient pagan polytheistic folk religion called Romuva is equally gaining momentum. The recently passed *krivis* (high priest) of the movement, Jonas Trinkunas, received the country's highest civilian honors for his dissident and religious work from the president of Lithuania. The movement is, like the Ásatrú Fellowship, currently building their first Romuva temple. Throughout Europe, similar spiritual expressions, such as the traditional folk-faith movements of Estonia and Finland, are appearing to reclaim their place. Whether these movements can transform themselves from mere historical curiosities to a lived reality remains to be seen.

Outside of the conventional spheres of spirituality, new voices are also arising in the realms of art. Poets, musicians, singers, filmmakers, writers, and painters are all drawing their visions from mythic wellsprings of ages past into the present and beyond, echoing simultaneously in their works the archaic and the futuristic. Art is the most fertile soil from which soul emerges. Art approximates ritual, which acts as an analogy of the world and a creation of new ones.

All of these things were shining beacons of spirit in a soulless age.

As I traveled across Europe, occasionally I encountered my friends—fellow travelers whom I had met at the sacred fires of India. With each of them I partook in rituals and shared libations, which took us back to our adventures in that extraordinary world. We had all encountered something far removed from what passes as normal life and reality. In these experiences, we were and would remain brothers and sisters. We were united by a great quest and a great story, ever unfolding, ever changing.

It was Easter when I met Vijaya, Lars, and their son, Merlin, whom I had gotten to know through our initiation into the magical tradition of India many years ago. The setting sun shone on my friends' faces as we stood on a tumulus (ancient grave mound) in a little village in the German countryside where they had made their home. On the mound dating back thousands of years stood a massive linden tree of some eight hundred years of age. Under its timeworn branches I said an old pagan prayer and raised a horn with my friends. We smiled in silence, and even the little boy Merlin put his face into the horn. As I concluded my words, the village church bells started chiming, their tolls reverberating through the quiet streets. All around us, barren fields of early spring turned golden in the fading evening sunlight.

A month or so later in Paris, summer was already in full bloom. I found myself again under the old statue of the great god Pan in Jardin du Luxembourg, watching my friend Christian approach. Somehow it was auspicious to meet here, at the feet of an ancient goat god of a wild untamed nature, so much like Shiva. We wandered through the bustling city, reflecting on life since our paths had crossed many years ago in the esoteric world of India and then under the most fateful of conditions—initiation and the death of our parents. But now life had returned anew. Christian had a wife and child and owned a yoga school in Paris. Arriving on the banks of the Seine, we finally opened a bottle of whiskey by the river, as we said we would do so many years before in what now seemed like a distant land and time. The river bore witness to our words and libations and carried them on.

When one crosses paths with kindred spirits outside of the ordinary, that is also the place where all future encounters will take place. Perhaps the true gifts of pilgrimage are those rare companions one meets during the journey, who are also searching intensly and who are also on a path toward the same elusive end.

At the autumnal conclusion of a month-long pilgrimage through the sacred sites in Europe with my lover, I found myself returning closer to my homeland. For the first time in my life, I had arrived at the landscape connected to my dream of so many years past, to the mounds of the god Frey at Gamla Uppsala, Sweden. At this central cultic site of an ancient temple of which only woodcuts have been preserved, the ancestral god himself was reputedly buried. Connected to this temple was a sacred grove with a large evergreen tree and a well—both used for a great blót, which occurred every nine years over a period of nine days. Throughout the ages it has been a high holy place, its soil drenched with blood, offerings, and ritual toasts. A row of stark burial mounds are now all that remain, breaking the otherwise flat landscape with their colossal presence. A church stands where reputedly a pagan temple had once stood.

As we approached, the mounds were silent. We saw no other people, save for the occasional lonely figure in the distance, tiny in comparison to the majestic hills. The sky was a hazy gray, although there was a strange glow in the air emanating from an unknown source. Trees stood motionless. All was still, holding its breath as if waiting for something.

There are three larger god mounds in old Uppsala. They are called the "royal mounds," and each is connected to one of the three divinities—Odin, Thor, and Frey.

Fig. 9.2. Uppsala mounds, Sweden
(Photograph by Justine Cederberg)

As we ascended to the top of the first one, the mound of Odin, a wind arose. Drops of rain suddenly started to fall, and two large black birds flew against the stark gray sky. From on top of the mound, views opened in all directions. I raised a drinking horn and said: "To the Allfather, the All-Knower." We poured some of the contents of the horn on the ground as an offering and consumed the rest.

As we climbed the second mound, the mound of Thor, the rain grew heavier. Again, I raised my voice in a toast: "To the sky forger, the thunder god."

By the time we made our way down from the second mound and up to the top of the third and last one—the mound of Frey, the ancestral god—the wind and rain had grown into a storm. As I raised my voice again, I was forced to shout: "To the ancestral god of the grave mound, the lord of earth!"

The rain poured down mercilessly, lashing our soaked figures standing boldly against the tempest high on the mound. With water stinging my face, the wet earth under my feet, I howled my words, which merged with the fury of the rising storm:

> *"Gods and goddesses!*
> *Forefathers and foremothers!*
> *Brothers and sisters!*
> *Both present and far away—hear us!*
> *Hear us cloaked in your sun and shadow and be with us*
>     *here at the edge of worlds!*
> *Protect our path and bless our blood—for from the same*
>     *source does our path spring and our blood from the*
>     *same fountain!*
> *We raise this toast to you, and we hail you!*
> *Share with us this libation for wisdom, for might, for joy,*
>     *for life!*
> *Bless us on this journey that has started but never ends!"*

Then, something opened up for me. A whirling well of memory was unveiled, containing remembrances beyond my own. My normal, smaller self dissolved into the air. As the wind cried and the rain poured, beating down ever harder, something else emerged. I no longer felt the wind, the rain, or the cold—all I felt was heat coursing in my blood. Here at the grave mounds of slumbering gods and kings, at this place of sacrifice, something stirred within my soul, a fury of ancient flames. And it emerged, ageless yet eternally youthful, life and death intertwined, awe, power, poetry—in a word, ecstasy. My being was a vessel for a force in flight, far beyond the ordinary. A god drunkenness came over me. I was carried on the wings of a part of my soul rarely touched, now soaring. My words *were* the wind, my being *was* the storm. For a moment on that mound, the gods were made flesh *in me*.

The instant we descended from the mound, the rain receded and the wind withdrew. It was as it had been before, quiet and calm. Walking away, I was soaking wet but warm from the afterglow of a state that had moved me to my very core. I turned back to look at the ancient mounds. They stood as before—silent monoliths against the forbidding sky.

Later, as I was pondering the state I had entered, I randomly opened a book on northern European tradition—and there it was, on the first page I glanced at. In the magical worldview of the old North, there is a component of the soul called the *wode*. It is the ecstatic state known to ancient peoples that allows one to be in touch with the world of the divinities, however briefly. This otherwise dormant part of the soul was what had for me flowered into sudden, forceful being on top of the fateful mounds.

Back in my ancestral house in the forest, I am surrounded by an all-devouring twilight. Only in the hearth is there a fire burning. Now, as it gets ever darker, and the world slips into ever-gloomier night, I turn to the blaze inside, to the embers of a flame waiting to be reborn. For there is a fire that never goes out.

I do not know whether the gods are faces that we give to that which is faceless in order to comprehend it and be close to it as human beings; if they are manifestations of distinct powers arising from an unknowable immensity or supreme reality or a oneness; if they are mediators or messengers between us and the god who is beyond comprehension; if they are aspects of nature and the world personified; if they are archetypes or forces of consciousness both within and without man; or if they are the highest human expressions of being beyond mortality. Perhaps they are a combination of all of the above.

What I do know is that the gods are mysteries and that we as human beings are ultimately drawn to them. And I know that they respond if one calls out to them. In times when the shrouds between worlds are temporarily unveiled, when our universe expands, they make themselves manifest. For this to happen one has to live poetically and live strongly. One has to live a life of great deeds, of overcoming—a life worthy of divine attention. One has to boldly face great sorrow and greater joy, for the gods have no interest in dull normalcy. Infinite divinities await, hidden within man himself—which is always the place of the final pilgrimage.

The godlike becomes living reality when dreams intersect with the waking world. These are knife-edge moments when the mythic cuts through the temporal to reveal the timeless, where the spirit is elevated to its superior states, where the poetic takes flight over the rational. In moments such as these, the gods awaken and reclaim their seat in the soul. We can hear them when we call out for them—in the crash of thunder and in the whisper of rustling leaves; in the creak of frosted, towering evergreens and in the roar of waves; in the solemn songs of eternal dawn and in the ecstatic cries of battle and love. And we wait for the furore of their return.

# GLOSSARY

**aarti:** A Hindu ritual where fire is offered to the deities.

**Adi Nath:** "First Lord," a name for the god Shiva.

**Aesir:** In the Norse pantheon the race of gods that includes Odin, Balder, and Thor and who live in Asgård.

**Aghori:** Shaivite sadhus known for their extreme spiritual practices, which include breaking social and religious taboos of purity to realize the nondualistic nature of the supreme being.

**akhara:** An order of the Sannyasi tradition; also a wrestling ring or a gymnasium where Indian martial arts are practiced.

**amrit:** Nectar of Immortality.

**Ardhanarishvara:** Hermaphrodite form of Shiva, a composite form of both Shiva and his wife Parvati.

**bhajan:** Devotional Hindu song.

**bhakti:** Devotion to a personal god or spiritual idea within the Indian religious traditions.

**Bholenath:** A name of Shiva as "kindhearted lord" and "lord of intoxicants"; usually invoked before smoking charas.

**bindu:** Point. It is usually a colored devotional dot that is put on the "third eye" of a devotee within the context of Hindu ritual.

**blót:** In the Norse pagan tradition a sacrifice made in honor of gods, spirits, or ancestors.

**blótgoda:** A name given to the Norse god Frey, which means "sacrifice priest"; he is the god who receives sacrifices and, in return, grants blessings.

**charas:** Hashish, handmade cannabis, common in India and Nepal.

**chela:** Disciple.

**chillum:** Indian pipe for smoking hashish used religiously by sadhus.

**chimtas:** Tongs used to tend the ritual fire of the dhuni.

**damaru:** Double-headed, hourglass-shaped hand drum often used in traditional Indian ritual.

**darshan:** The "beholding," a revealing and personal experience of the sacred or divine presence; derives from the Sanskrit root *drsh*, "to see."

**Demiurge:** In gnostic tradition, a false ruler and creator of the imperfect material world.

**dhuni:** Sacred fire, usually a fire pit.

**Fenrir:** In the Norse mythology, the giant wolf who is foretold to kill Odin during Ragnarök; one of Loki's children.

**Fimbulvinter:** In Norse mythology, the long winter preceding Ragnarök, the twilight of the gods.

**Frey:** Meaning "lord," Frey is one of the main gods of the Norse pantheon. Associated with earth, prosperity, peace, sacrifice, sacred kingship, and ancestry, he is originally part of the Vanir race or group of gods.

**Freya:** Twin sister to Frey, she is goddess of war, *seiðr* sorcery, love, and sexuality, who is responsible for teaching Odin himself the secrets of magic.

**ganas:** Shiva's wild entourage of chthonic creatures.

**gangajal:** Water from the holy Ganga river.

**ghanta:** Ritual bell.

**ghat:** A flight of steps leading to a body of water.

**gopis:** Lovers and devotees of the god Krishna; in Hindu mythology the gopis were milkmaids who fell in love with the young Krishna when he was a *gopala,* or cowherd, in Vrindavan.

**gunas:** The three innate qualities of Prakriti, nature, which are *rajas* (active), *tamas* (passive), *sattva* (balance).

**guru:** Spiritual teacher, "the one who dispels darkness."

**guru bhais:** Spiritual brothers united by the same guru.

**havan:** Ancient Vedic fire ritual.

**Hel:** In the Norse pantheon she is the goddess of one realm of the dead; one of Loki's children.

**hof:** Old Norse word for a temple building within Germanic religion.

**Ilmarinen:** In the Finnish pantheon he is the sky forger, "eternal hammerer," and blacksmith who forges the mythic artifact of the Sampo.

**Iormungandr:** In the Norse pantheon Iormungandr is the Midgård sea serpent who encircles the entire earth and gnaws on his tail like Ouroboros; he is a child of Loki and the giantess Angrboda.

**jata:** Matted locks of hair often seen on sadhus.

**jötunn:** In the Norse pantheon the jötunn are a race of giants who have a complex relationship with the gods.

**Juna Akhara:** The ancient order of the Renunciates of the Ten Names; Juna Akhara is the largest and oldest order of sadhus in India.

**kalari:** Training hall and shrine of the practitioners of kalaripayat, an ancient southern Indian martial art.

**kalaripayat:** Ancient southern Indian martial art.

**kama:** Desire.

**kamandal:** Water pot used by sadhus.

**kantele:** Finnish and Karelian stringed instrument connected to the god, hero, and singer of magic runes, Väinämöinen, "the eternal sage." When Väinämöinen leaves his people at the advent of Christianity, he gifts the future generations with his kantele.

**kapala:** A bowl made out of a human skull used in Hindu rituals.

**Kumbh Mela:** A great spiritual fair within the Hindu tradition and the largest gathering of people for a spiritual, magical, or religious purpose on planet Earth.

**Kundalini:** Serpent goddess and consort of Shiva who gives her name to name to a coiled energy, or shakti, at the base of the spine, the ascension of which signifies the merging of the subjective with the objective.

**Líf and Lífþrasir:** In Norse mythology "Life" and "Life-lust," the two humans, female and male respectively, who will again populate the Earth after Ragnarök.

**lingoti:** Loincloth worn by sadhus.

**Louhi:** In Finnish mythology, queen and witch of the North as well as enemy of Väinämöinen.

**maithuna:** Sacred sexual union in a ritual context.

**mala:** Garland of prayer beads.

**mandir:** Hindu temple.

**mleccha:** Ancient Indian term for foreigner and barbarian.

**mudra:** Hindu ritual gesture, often made with hands or fingers.

**muladhara chakra:** Root chakra of seven chakras in the Hindu tradition.

**Naga Baba:** Shaivite sadhu ascetic belonging to the Naga Baba order.

**Nandikeshwara:** A name and form of Shiva.

**Nataraja:** Shiva in his form as "lord of the dance."

**Navratri:** "Festival of Nine Nights" celebrating the Goddess in her various forms.

**Nilakantha:** Shiva in his form as the drinker of poisons, "the blue-throated one."

**Njörðr:** Old Norse sea god, father of Frey and Freya.

**Odin:** The Allfather of the Germanic spiritual traditions; seeker of wisdom, finder of runes, god of poetry, ecstasy, magic, and war.

**panch guru initiation:** "The initiation of five gurus" needed to become a Naga Sannyasi.

**Pashupati:** Shiva in his form as lord of animals.

**Prakriti:** Hindu concept of nature, which consists of three *gunas* or innate qualities.

**prasad:** "That which pleases," an often sweet food (such as fruit or nuts) that is first offered to the gods in Hindu ritual and, when the gods are pleased, distributed among the devotees.

**puja:** Ritual in the Hindu tradition.

**Punarvasu:** A lunar mansion in Hindu astrology.

**Puranas:** Ancient Hindu scriptures.

**Purusha:** Universal man or supreme soul or consciousness, witness to Prakriti.

**puttara:** Seven-tiered platform or altar in a kalari.

**Ragnarök:** In Norse mythology the cataclysmic events that will bring an end to both gods and men, "twilight of the gods."

**rishis:** Sages of the Vedas.

**Rudra:** Shiva in his least compassionate form, "the howler."

**sadhana:** Spiritual practice.

**sadhu:** Mystic ascetic, renunciate monk, or wandering holy man in the Hindu tradition.

**Sakhi:** Transvestite lovers and devotees of Krishna (also known as gopis); the Sakhi are men who dress as women in order to be as close as possible to their lord.

**Sampo:** In Finnish mythology the Sampo is the mysterious magical artifact that produces good fortune and prosperity.

**sampradaya:** Initiatory tradition.

**sannyasa:** Renunciate.

**satsang:** Spiritual teachings, usually in person with a guru or a group of students.

**seiðr:** In old Norse religion a type of sorcery or shamanic magic; mythically connected with Freya and Odin.

**shakti:** Power, strength, primordial cosmic energy.

**Shakti:** Consort of Shiva; the goddess representing the energy of life that animates Purusha, supreme consciousness.

**Shankara:** A name of Shiva in his form as the primordial yogi.

**tapasvin:** A practitioner of austerities.

**tapasya:** Physical and spiritual yogic austerities practiced to light the inner fire, or *tapas,* and gain recognition from the gods.

**Thangka:** Tibetan and Nepalese tradition of elaborate painting on cotton or silk appliqué, depicting Hindu or Tibetan Buddhist deities or mandalas. More than mere decorative art, Thangkas have a function in ritual, meditation, and monastic life.

**Thor:** In the Norse pantheon Thor is the mighty god of thunder who wields a hammer called Mjölnir.

**tirtha:** Holy place, "crossing over place."

**trishul:** Indian word for trident, a three-headed spear carried by gods such as Shiva and Durga as well as the Naga Babas.

**urdhvabahu:** Sadhus who keep their arm raised as a tapasya until it stiffens in such a position.

**Väinämöinen:** In the Finnish pantheon Väinämöinen is the powerful god of magic, seeker of wisdom, and singer of the runes (runos), often described as an old man.

**vanaprastha:** Hermit, one who has "retired into the woods"; also relates to the third of the four stages of Hindu life.

**Vanir:** In Norse pantheon the Vanir are the race or group of gods who come from Vanaheim but live in Asgård; this group includes Frey and Freya.

**vibhuti:** Sanskrit word for sacred ritual ash.

**vritti:** A term in yoga for the fluctuations or waves of the mind, which yoga aims to silence.

**wode:** A component of the soul in the magical worldview of the old North. It is the ecstatic state that allows contact with the world of the divinities.

**yatra:** Pilgrimage.